LIFE ABOVE THE LINE

LIFE ABOVE THE LINE

LIVING THE LIFE
YOU'RE MEANT TO LIVE

TIFFANY GARVIN

Silver Torch Press
Beverly Hills, CA

Life Above the Line: Living the Life You're Meant to Live

Copyright © 2016 by Tiffany Garvin

www.TiffanyGarvin.co
LifeAboveTheLine@gmail.com

 Published by Silver Torch Press
www.SilverTorchPress.com
jill@SilverTorchPress.com

ISBN: 978-1-942707-37-0
LCCN: 2016953003

Cover and back design by Tiffany Garvin.
Edited by Sarah Moffitt.

Printed in the United States of America.

"Your perspective is always limited by how much you know. Expand your knowledge and you will transform your mind."

~ Bruce Lipton

SPECIAL THANKS

I am so grateful for this amazing work that I'm privileged to share. I'm thankful for the healing I've experienced and the new energy in my life. It's wonderful to see lives changing and people thriving though using these beautiful techniques. I am also grateful for the countless hours of help to produce this book.

Thank you Sarah Jensen for being so generous with your time as I worked through my thoughts.

Thank you Tammy Anderson Ward for being inspired to be my mentor and motivating me to finish this book.

Thank you Shane Thomson for sharing your gifts and the powerful brainstorming sessions.

Thank you Craig Boucher for believing in me and understanding the soul of this book. You and Connie are my guardian angels.

I am grateful to my kids Sterling, Connery and Keeley for being my test subjects over the years with this work. You've definitely brought me lots of challenges to resolve. You're amazing!

I especially appreciate my loving, enduring, inspired and handsome husband, Chris. Thank you for believing in my dreams and giving me wings to fly! I love you tons!

To you, the reader, thank you for following the promptings to pick up this book and explore its pages. I know your life will be blessed, you'll find answers to some of your greatest challenges and you will be able to overcome the obstacles to becoming who you are meant to become and living your powerful purpose!

TABLE OF CONTENTS

FOREWORD

I admire Tiffany for her courage and willingness to write this book to bless the lives of others. It's difficult for many to revisit past hardships, let alone write a book about them. It's clear that her desire is to give credit to the true Master Healer, Jesus Christ.

These days, Alternative Health therapies are becoming more and more popular. Why? They are effective a good majority of the time and have little to no side effects, have minimal cost compared to surgeries or other expensive medical care, and put people in charge of their own path.

I have been blessed to experience the incredible feeling that comes through being self reliant. I too feel a strong duty to others in connecting them with effective, Christ-centered resources, one reason I created the well attended Christ-centered Energy Healing Conferences. Tiffany is a frequent speaker, and her teaching style is very effective. Through Tiffany's authentic, loving, and simple approach, she's been able to teach and help countless people.

Reading this book will take you on a journey to the *light* of the world. Those who delve into the energy healing world are like a neon sign. They don't point at themselves; rather they show others the way, pointing toward Jesus. I am a champion for Jesus. I love Him with all of my heart. I know Tiffany feels the same way. When you are in her presence you can feel her immense gratitude for all the experiences and knowledge she has acquired, coupled with her sincere desire to show others how to heal.

Tammy Anderson Ward
Founder, Hope Haven Event

INTRODUCTION

*"The future belongs to those who
believe in the beauty of their dreams."*

~Eleanor Roosevelt

Each person on earth has a powerful path that is perfect for their growth and joy. Our challenges, trials, and struggles are designed to teach and even empower us. As we learn to glean these lessons from our lives—and then *heal* them—we can become who we're meant to become and do what we are meant to do. We can live a *life above the line.*

I've been there. When I was sick, I tried seemingly everything. Then at last, I discovered this work. This amazing yet simple system holds the answers that I've searched for across an 18-year-long healing journey. With the simple techniques you'll learn in these pages, I am able to manage every physical, mental, emotional, and life challenge that comes to me. I learn the lessons of life more easily and effectively than ever before. I am happier, healthier, and enjoying my life like I never thought possible. I wrote this book because I want that for you too!

This book is a hands-on, practical, and hopefully inspiring introduction to the *Perfect Healing©* System and the *Life above the Line* philosophy. You'll learn the basics needed to begin making significant shifts in your health, happiness, and success. The techniques are simple, but their effects are life-changing. In this small but profound book, you will gain a new depth of understanding about the principles and philosophies that illuminate the path for mental, emotional, physical, social, and spiritual healing.

There's no magical, comprehensive answer to all of life's problems. No one technique, method or modality will help everyone heal from every physical ailment, resolve every emotional burden or make everyone financially wealthy. What is possible, however, is to learn the universal principles regarding your challenge and then find the method that resonates with you. The universal principles are consistent, but how they manifest and are applied to your struggles can be modified to help you more easily resolve them.

The personal development and healing modality of the *Perfect Healing©* System may not be the answer to everyone's challenges, but its simple and profound techniques are accessible to all who desire it to bless their lives. Give yourself a real chance. Explore this introduction to the *Perfect Healing©* System and discover for yourself the universal principles that will help you solve your greatest challenges.

Diligent use of these techniques healed me from 18 years of chronic illnesses. I had to try a dozen different methods before discovering my treasure trove of healing. But once it appeared, I overcame pain, fatigue, and even self-critical beliefs. This difficult search for answers to life's challenges is a common plague. I am excited to share with you how easily you can find your answers within you.

In this book, you will find philosophy, principles, and techniques that will show you how to approach your life in a new and empowered way. The simplicity and power that lies herein will show you the power within *you* to improve your health, happiness and success. You will learn how to live your *life above the line*. You will learn how to overcome the obstacles to becoming who you are meant to become and doing what you are meant to do.

Life above the line is a new approach to personal development and healing. It highlights the innate capacities in all of us to solve our own problems. It takes the mystery out of self-healing and achieving goals. It's so simple and yet so powerful that your only challenge will be that you might underestimate its potential for influence in your life. Don't make that mistake. Engage fully and trust the process. *You* have more power than you realize.

Some of my clients and students have amazed me with their own healing. One has helped herself heal from hypersensitivities to food, another has eliminated stress-related trips to the emergency room, and others have overcome chronic depression and trauma. I'm humbled and grateful to see what they have accomplished as they've learned these beautiful techniques. I believe you can have this kind of success as well. What challenge are you struggling with that these techniques can help you overcome? What limiting beliefs and fears do you have that are preventing you from achieving your greatest desires?

The wisdom in this book will show you how to access your innate gifts and power to help yourself heal from illness, trauma, stress, allergies, and much more. Discover the power of being your own best problem solver and taking charge of your health, happiness, and success.

CHAPTER 1

LIFE ABOVE THE LINE

*"Grant me the strength to focus this week,
to be mindful and present,
to serve with excellence, to be a force of love."*

~ *Brendon Burchard*

Living a *life above the line* is a reality we can all experience. We are meant to live with joy, to create and thrive, and to become a better version of ourselves. When this is our reality, we are living *above the line*. However, life can offer us opportunities for growth that, on the surface, appear as tragedy, trauma and struggle. These masked gifts can take us *below the line* and cause us pain, but they are meant to help us build and become who we are meant to become. In their unique ways, trials are clues and even blessings that can show us what we are meant to do in this life.

Life and its trials are not as unpredictable as we might believe, and discovering the answers to our problems is not as mysterious as we have come to accept. There's a predictable cycle that our lives follow and we can influence it; in fact, we influence it constantly. The question you need to ask is how you are influencing your life. Just look around and you will see what patterns you are perpetuating. Your current challenges are there as a mirror of what's inside of you. The great thing about this is that if you're not pleased with where you are, you can begin changing it immediately.

Our lives exhibit a spiraling effect that is actually a pattern in nature. It is called the Fibonacci Sequence. Mathematically, it is a series of numbers that builds and creates a beautiful spiral. We see it very clearly in the nautilus shell, as the center spiral is small and tight and then grows bigger as it moves outward.

This natural design also has practical application in our lives as a pattern of creation *and* a pattern of healing. The image below illustrates what we're talking about. The spiral represents the progression of our lives, with "The Line" representing the very real moment where we make a shift in our experience, whether into a mode of creating or merely surviving. The progression dips below the line and rises up in repeating cycles until it creates this grand and beautiful spiral. Our lives can be our own unique, exquisite creation of joy, meaning, and powerful gifts to share with the world. This predictable pattern also helps us understand our lives better and be better able to experience and move through life more effectively, and ultimately, more happily.

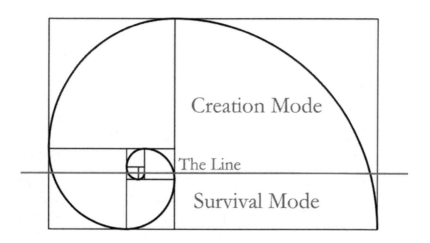

Creation Mode

The Line

Survival Mode

Moving Above the Line is a natural, healthy progression in life. We are meant to live with joy. *Life above the line* is living in creation mode—inventing and enjoying life. It is bright, hopeful, and positive. Here, reacting to life's challenges is productive and empowering, not paralyzing. Life is manageable, not overwhelming. Success is attainable and anticipated. Life is meaningful and satisfying. We are discovering and developing our innate gifts and learning how to serve the world with them. We recognize our value and that of people around us. We spread this powerful permission to shine to all we encounter.

Living below the line is like living in a whirlpool, swirling around, trying to stay afloat. It is constant struggle. Hope is harder to come by. Success feels nearly impossible. People often feel like the victims in their own lives instead of the heroes of their stories. Under the line, it's difficult to see a way out of their challenges. Their burdens weigh them down, often leading to mental and emotional paralysis.

As we make the mindset change and begin activating our inner strength and power, we move upward, toward the line. We can push through and work to heal what has kept us below the line. As we overcome these obstacles, we rise above the line. We begin feeling relief and see the possibilities of living without paralyzing burdens. Then we feel encouraged and recognize our power to really change. We start dreaming and creating and even see some success. As we become stronger, we get to see more things that need to be healed. We accept those as lessons to learn, grow, and heal from. We heal those and continue to build.

The cycle continues. We heal more of what's below the line, and then rise up in strength. We happily accept what baggage surfaces and clear it away—we heal it and then rise again. Each time we acknowledge and work on what comes up, the healing is deeper and more profound. Then, when we rise above the line, we're higher and stronger.

Obviously, the sequence of our lives is not so clean and simple. While we may be above the line in some aspects of life, we find ourselves below the line in others. What's important is that we recognize where we are in relation to the line in any given facet of our lives—are we in creation or survival mode?—and respond accordingly. That is the purpose of the *Perfect Healing©* System: to help us heal all that brings us below the line so that we can live our lives in full creation mode above the line and become all that we are meant to be.

This whole book is about moving from where you are to a better place, being happier, healthier, and more successful in life. With the tools you will learn here, you'll be able to feel more energy and motivation, more hope and clarity. You will become empowered to make changes in your life in order to feel the relief and peace that you've been craving.

As you read, begin recognizing the patterns in your life. Pay attention to the thoughts that come regarding patterns to change, goals to reach for, and dreams to pursue. There are lessons to learn right in front of you. Recognize where you are in the cycle. Are you swirling below the line? Are you pushing through the line into creation mode?

In the next chapter, I will share with you a bit of my story. You'll see how my journey took me below the line and how I began to change that. This is the beginning of a new journey in *your* life. With the tools in this book, you will begin moving from survival mode to creation mode. Create your wish list—those things that you want to improve and build in your life. You can do this. There is a reason you found this book. This is your time!

CHAPTER 2

THE WORST PAIN OF MY LIFE

"Make no small plans,
they have no magic to stir men's souls."

~ Unknown

At only 22 years old, I should have had an amazing life ahead of me right? But what was happening to me? The doctor just informed me that I would likely be dealing with intense pain and debilitating fatigue for the rest of my life. I felt lost, confused. Worse than that, most of the people around me thought I was faking it. *Are you kidding me?!* All I wanted was to do what I had been sent there to do, but there I was, thousands of miles from home, living with a stranger of a roommate, and in the worst pain of my life.

I was a missionary for my church, a great 18-month adventure far from home, and I *knew* the Lord wanted me there. Missions come with lots of blessings and lots of trials. My first weekend at the training facilities, I got the flu. *No big deal*, I thought, *just part of the experience.* Within a day or so I felt better, but soon after that, I suddenly lost my voice. Getting sick the first time had me already feeling a little awkward around my assigned training group, and there I was, sick again. Then the lost voice turned into back pain—totally not normal. My trainer helped me coordinate some visits to a local chiropractor, hoping to help me get some relief. The adjustments seemed to help, so a few weeks later

I was sent out to my first area to start working, this time even farther away from home.

During the first few days, my back felt weak and only mildly achy, so I didn't think much about it, but the life of a missionary includes walking and teaching and serving for many hours each day, and the pain was increasing. There is a culture among missionaries of giving your all, holding nothing back in the service of the Lord and others and if someone is struggling to live up to that standard—especially without visible cause—it can be confusing and frustrating, so I guess it's not surprising that my new companion/teaching partner seemed a little impatient with my struggles and even a bit argumentative about us keeping the pace. I tried to explain that I *was* doing my best but that something was wrong and I didn't know what it was. There *may* be some people who just can't handle the workload, but *that* wasn't me.

The days wore on and the pain increased. I felt my energy diminishing until one morning, I was completely exhausted and I could hardly get out of bed. At this point I really started to worry. Here I was, thousands of miles from home, deteriorating for no apparent reason, and scared. I received permission from our mission leader to go to a doctor. One medical appointment turned into several as no one could figure out what was going on. They poked and prodded and tested, but the doctors didn't know what to do with me. They made their guesses, but the numerous tests they ran amounted to no more than circumstantial evidence that it was probably all in my head; that's what they told my leaders, and that's when it got ugly.

My mission leader was now convinced that I was just a problematic youth trying to get out of something. He lectured me sternly and told me to get back to work. He also informed me that my companion had told him I was trouble. This stunned me. I was dealing with massive pain, intense fatigue, and now betrayal. I was terrified, and for the first time in my life, truly angry.

When I saw my companion next, she received the best go-to-heck look I could give. It must have been good because she stepped back; I think she realized she had messed up.

With new disdain and renewed determination, I said I would do whatever we needed to do. This meant a lot of walking in whatever weather was to be had—rain, cold, etc.—so out we went. By the time we were done with that day of work, pushing as hard as I could, I collapsed. My companion had to carry me to the car to head home and then practically carry me into the apartment. I was shattered. Suddenly, she could see the truth: I was really sick.

My companion helped me get to another doctor, a kindhearted Internist. She said she had an idea of what was going on—finally!—but that it was bad news. She stopped short of giving a diagnosis, but if it was what she suspected, it would be a life sentence of misery. The good news was that my companion and one of the other missionaries in our group finally believed me. Everyone else that mattered, however, was convinced of my tenacious deception and made my life incredibly difficult.

Shortly thereafter, bad turned to worse. In our weekly missionary training meetings, I had easily memorized and retained numerous scriptures and teaching materials. I was very good at it. Then, one day, it just stopped. It was bizarre and disturbing; I couldn't retain more than a sentence. My short-term memory had suddenly turned off and I was almost paralyzed with fear. All of the pressure, the mocking, the threats to get back to work, and now this made me think I was losing my mind. I just wanted to find out what was wrong, take care of it, and finish what I was there to do, but it was hopeless. Impatience surrounded me and the doubts in my mind were leading me toward the loony bin.

Like a ray of light shining through the dark clouds, my mom swung in and pulled me out of the pit. She called me unexpectedly one day after speaking with the mission leader. Something I had written in a letter a few days earlier had her worried, so she was just checking back in with my mission leader, and the person he described to her didn't sound like the daughter she knew at all. So at just the right time, she called my apartment and pulled me out of the terrified stupor I was in, helping me muster up the strength to face my situation. I met with the mission leader, where he gave me the option to stay or to go home. I had given everything to make it work, and I could see that it was just not going to work after all. Only a few weeks into my 18-month assignment, I told him I was ready to go home.

Within a few days I was on a plane and headed back home to a safe, nurturing, albeit confused family. After picking me up and seeing a withered, pale, sickly version of the daughter my parents had sent out to serve a mission, they were stunned and quickly shifted gears. While they strategized how to unravel the mystery of my sudden decline in health, I wondered what would come of me. Would I ever feel good again? I love to learn, but would I get to return to college to finish my degree? Would anyone want to marry this invalid I had turned into? These questions haunted me as I struggled beneath the weight of constant, mind-numbing pain in my back, a non-existent short-term memory, paralyzing fatigue, and a host of other random symptoms.

As if the new illness was not enough, I now felt like a failure. We had spent hundreds of dollars, massive faith, and months preparing for my mission, and I had wasted it all. I was so sure that the mission was right— *knew* it was—but then somehow it suddenly wasn't. I had to face my failure as well as my family and neighbors who had been so excited for me. Even some of them questioned whether I was really sick, and it really hurt. I couldn't bear the judgment and questions. I was devastated.

The days and nights dragged on as I attempted to deal with the pain and to rest as well as I could. Being born into a strong, faith-filled family, we sought guidance through prayer. One day after a prayer that my father offered on my behalf, he told me he felt strongly that I would eventually get well. When I heard those words, I felt something too. It was almost as if the pain in my body recognized that this was a temporary stop. I took the words as a literal message from heaven. That day began the greatest treasure hunt of my life, and I knew that I would eventually be healthy again. It was just a matter of faith and time.

I want you to experience this shift in your own life. The power is inside of you. The techniques you will learn in this book will facilitate a powerful change within you and around you. You will be able to benefit from this beautiful treasure that I discovered through my life- and body-healing journey. After 18 years, my healing quest was finally complete. The constant pain is gone. My energy is restored. I feel capable once again to live a life of my choosing. That's what this book is about—how my life changed, and how yours can too.

CHAPTER 3

HOPE

*"Once you choose hope,
anything is possible"*

~ *Christopher Reeve*

In my current role as a health and life mentor, I see people everywhere struggling with more and more physical, mental, and emotional issues that don't seem to have answers or cures. They come to me with what little hope they have left in them to feel better. Their lives are screaming at them for relief, peace—*change*—but they can't seem to find it. The illness or challenge begins simply as a frustration or handful of symptoms and then turns into a several-year battle that strains them emotionally and financially—often leaving emotional scars to match their surgical ones. No matter how many doctors, therapists, or seminars they've gone to that left them disappointed and financially depleted, we work to resolve each challenge, and their journey turns from despair to a lighted path of hope and resolution. In one way or another, you have been there. I've been there too, and I know the way out.

The holy scriptures highlight a problem I see often that men's hearts are failing them. I see it in a literal sense when hearts are broken from tragedy or long-term pressure. I see it in people giving up on feeling better. I see it when people lose their nerve to go after a dream. I see it in fear- filled eyes about a future that seems hopeless. These struggles are real. These sweet people are trying their hardest to survive a difficult economy and support their families. They are giving their all to find peace in a chaotic world. They hold onto a precious ounce of hope that someday they will feel true joy. They see promises all around them for greater health, happiness, and financial abundance, but they no longer feel the courage to try and risk being disappointed again. I can see it too because I lived it; it's been my pain too.

THE TREASURE IS REAL!

I can see this clearly because I lived it. My parents spent thousands of dollars that they didn't really have in working to find relief for me. I went along, willing to try anything and everything. There were medications, crazy diets, unusual treatments, and dozens of trips to a variety of practitioners. Each new attempt offered hope, but none of them offered the answers I was searching for. Months and years went by. Eventually, most of them would provide some relief. Sometimes the relief even lasted for a while. Still, my treasure—my cure—was ever elusive.

Finally, after what felt like a lifetime of searching, I found it. I saw the pot of gold at the end of the rainbow and ran! These techniques that I use on myself and my clients are that treasure. Sometimes I feel like Dorothy from the Wizard of Oz, because I had it all along. The awareness and understanding on how to apply it came just recently and has already produced several miracles. I am healthy! I can live my life without physical limitations. No more endless and terrifying pain! No more debilitating fatigue! I'm still working on my memory, but hey, nobody's perfect! I feel true, deep, profound joy about my journey and the beautiful lessons that I've learned along the way and I'm so excited to share how I did it and how anyone can do it.

Now that my health is stable and improving, I'm freer than

ever to move above that line that once taunted my limitations of activities and dreams. I can manage my health beautifully and I feel energy, drive, and excitement about living a life that's meaningful. I can explore my gifts, develop them, and serve with them. It's remarkable how much joy comes from sharing from my heart the gifts I've been given. Who knew that I had so much in me to give! I want everyone to feel this!

THE TREASURE IS FOR EVERYONE

Something that I've realized along my path is that not only do I have a purpose for my life—gifts to share and joy to feel—but everyone has them too. Every human being on this planet has been blessed with gifts, talents, and abilities to use to help them accomplish a unique purpose in this life. We are all meant to serve the world in our own special way. This means that everyone is meant to be happy and have meaningful lives! It's possible!

This is why I do what I do. My journey of illness and struggle was not in vain. I was given an education that not only healed me and empowered me, but also taught me to see what my purpose is in this life. I am meant to help people move beyond their limitations of mental, emotional and physical health, and more so that they can accomplish their unique purposes in their lives. I know that the access to this healing power lies in everyone and I can't wait for them to realize it and transform their lives too. The answers are here and they are beautifully simple.

CHAPTER 4

THE USUAL EFFORTS

*"You are entitled to draw on the powers
of heaven in realizing any righteous desire,
be it emotionally, socially, professionally,
or academically oriented."*

~ Grant Von Harrison

My story is my story—totally unique to me. I hope that within my story, however, there are elements that many can relate to, particularly those who struggle with long, difficult challenges. This journey we all take to learn our life lessons and discover answers to our challenges allows us to travel both below and above the line, thus helping us become our best selves. I've been there and because of this, I know that what I've learned will help you too.

I've experienced some elements along my journey that may parallel some of what you have seen—seeking professional, non-professional, and even self-help resources. Some were more helpful than others, but they all taught me something. As we do what we know, we learn and then we do better and learn more; it's all a part of that healing journey.

PROFESSIONAL HELP

As a society, we usually seek traditional, professional help when we experience a difficult challenge. I did. We go to a doctor for our physical illnesses and injuries and take prescribed medications when needed. We get x-rays and surgeries, followed by help from therapists that specialize in our particular ailment. If the challenge is complicated enough, we may even bounce around from doctor's office to hospital to pharmacy and everywhere in between to try to take care of our physical needs. We will follow all of the instructions in hope of finding relief.

For psychological or emotional help, we will often find a counselor, psychologist or psychiatrist to help us feel better or think better. We hope that someone will know us better than we know ourselves. We trust that their years of experience will give us that one insight that we've been missing this whole time that will shift everything back into gear. Sometimes we get prescriptions from these types of doctors too. We hope they will balance the chemicals that are off or fix some neural connections that we're missing. We hope that there are answers out there; that it's just a matter of finding the right doctor to show it to us.

SOCIAL/NON-PROFESSIONAL HELP

Sometimes we find support from informal sources. I sought answers through this route when I wanted more than what the professional sector could provide.

We counsel with our families, chat with our friends, and even seek answers on social media. As the social creatures we are, we often find some relief through these channels. Everyone has had experiences with one thing or another. The firsthand experience of trusted sources is desirable, especially when these sources worked through the physical, mental, or emotional issue that we're going through. We also hope that because these people know us, they'll be able to help us fill in the gaps and find the answers that professionals might miss. These paths are often a bit less intimidating—not to mention free. We are inclined to help those we care about, so this non-professional course can hold a plethora of possible solutions.

SELF-HELP

There are those of us who are led to try to figure things out on our own. I tried this approach after the first two attempts at healing through professional and non-professional sources did all they could, but were still insufficient.

In looking for solutions, we all may go to support groups, seminars, social gatherings and a variety of events that promise solutions to all that ails us. We'll buy books, listen to audios, and study every piece of material that offers any amount hope. We take comfort in our efforts because others have figured things out in the past and hopefully they created some kind of product that we can learn from in order to figure things out for ourselves as well. Sometimes, we go the inward route to see what answers may already lay inside of us. We try meditating on our problems. We make it a matter of prayer to see what guidance we can find through a Divine source. Whether with help from a book like this one or some other way, we hope that we can finally take care of our problems ourselves.

CHAPTER 5

TYPICAL OUTCOMES

"Pain is inevitable, suffering is optional."

~ Haruki Murakami

Whatever pattern of searching we follow, we are met with a variety of outcomes. Sometimes we have a *Eureka!* moment—we find the solution and are on our way. Other times it's a flop and we wish we had left that option out of our plans. Usually, however, the results are mixed—we are kind of successful. Even when the attempted method for solving our challenge is less than productive, we may still gain something valuable. The journey is always filled with opportunities to learn, grow and sometimes reevaluate our decision-making skills. I experienced all of these and I learned from each one. What a blessing! There is always something good that comes from going through this kind of process. Here are some of the outcomes that our journeys often produce.

EUREKA!

We can hit the jackpot through any of these avenues. A doctor can prescribe just the right medication or treatment and we've got our lives back. A therapist can say something profound that hits our core and we're changed. A trusted friend can provide information about a miraculous method or product that solves our issue. We find the perfect thing on Facebook and we're cured! We master the lessons that came with our challenge and we continue our lives in joy. We move on to teach everyone who will listen about our amazing recovery and spread the blessings! We've done it!

KIND OF SUCCESSFUL

While that all sounds amazing, if you're reading this book, that probably hasn't happened to you yet. What's a bit more likely is that you've tried some things and had some success; you learned some good tools, had some positive results and felt hopeful. It may not have solved all your problems, but you were pleased to see something that worked. You share your newfound solution when someone mentions that you seem to be doing better. You're grateful for the acknowledgment and have a pleasant interaction. In the end, however, you're still dealing with your problem and are disappointed that you didn't find complete relief.

FLOP

Then there's the path you followed that seemingly led nowhere. You spent money that you felt accomplished nothing and now regret it. You had no results to speak of. No matter what you tried, nothing seemed to work. You felt frustrated and discouraged. Maybe you're even angry that you fell for that revolutionary method that's helping everybody else. You make sure you tell people what *didn't* work and you keep looking. You start feeling hopeless, discouraged. You wonder if the answer is really out there; or after trying so many things that haven't worked, if perhaps you will be stuck with this burden for the rest of your life. The downward spiral begins. Voices in your head seem to berate you and blame you for the failures you've experienced. "Stop trying." "It's not worth it." "Nothing is going to work." What do

21

you do now?

You go back to the drawing board because as much as there is discouragement and frustration swirling around inside of you, there is that little voice that tells you to keep going. Keep trying. You *will* find the answer. Everything will be alright. You take a deep breath and then read a quote on Facebook that says something like, "It's never win or *lose*, only win or *learn*." Something inside of you resonates with that quote and you feel a new spark of determination. The hunt is back on.

CHAPTER 6

MY TREASURE HUNT

*"Committed pursuit of goals gives us a sense
of mission, of pursuit, of being part of something
bigger than ourselves, and studies show that
this increases our sense of control over our lives,
which is known to affect the health of the body."*

~ Dr. Lissa Rankin

I experienced all of this to one degree or another, as I imagine you have as well. I found things that were kind of successful. I had my share of attempts that were total flops. I trudged through my share of excitement, frustration, hopelessness, and awe. And then, finally, I did have my *eureka*! Here's a bit more detail into my journey.

MEDICAL

My visits to medical doctors were very few. After a handful of what I like to call 'pin cushion' visits where they take blood and infuse some glowing liquid to see if they can figure out what's going on, the answers were scant and left even more questions. The doctors I went to said nothing about diet, exercise, stress, or anything other than medications. They told me to take anti-depressants and painkillers. Nothing was offered to help me overcome my health issues, just mask them. Well, they didn't work. I quickly realized that the medical world wasn't ready for my problems, so I shifted my focus and opened my mind wide open.

ALTERNATIVE/COMPLEMENTARY

Wow! I discovered that there's a whole world out there offering ways to support the body naturally. There are products, techniques, and modalities that strengthen the body and work with it to discover the root cause of a problem and focus efforts to address it. These alternative and complementary therapies more often than not consider the whole person instead of just a piece or two, attempting to account for all of the factors in illness. I found out that ignoring stress or the emotional factors in someone's physical illness is shortsighted and nearly always insufficient.

The more I worked on my physical struggles, the more I realized how small of a role the physical played in my ailments. The mental, emotional, and even spiritual aspects of life were more significantly impacting my health. When I tried changing my diet, it may have helped some, but I was already eating pretty healthy. I remember how helpful it was to keep as active as I could. When I just sat around in a puddle of pain and fatigue, I felt worse, so even though I couldn't move around a ton, I learned to sew, knit, and crochet. I think I made nearly 20 baby blankets in about 3 months, a few bridesmaids dresses—my little sister got married—and a host of other random projects just to keep my hands busy; it helped more than the pain medication.

Homeopathic remedies, specialized chiropractors, and some Chinese therapies seemed to help make some positive shifts in my health. It was around this time that my mind woke up. I had been in a kind of fog for a couple years by this point, so when I began thinking clearly again my mind was incredibly thirsty for knowledge. I checked out several different books from the library and read them all. I read anything from interior design and photography to political philosophy and more. I couldn't get enough information. After a few more months, I felt good enough to go back to college. I slowly, but surely made some headway toward my degree. Progress in my educational goals contributed to my improving health. I was feeling hope and a bit less pain.

A while later, I was able to participate in some martial arts training. At first I thought it was crazy, as I was still far from having a lot of energy, but I couldn't deny the clear signs that this was my next step. In the beginning, I was slow and careful, timid to exert myself very much. Slowly and steadily, however, I began to gain strength. My pain eased and I was feeling more energy. My classes were motivating and uniquely nurturing given the small and special arrangements. It was me, three new Kenpo brothers, and an instructor that cared for us like his own kids. They welcomed me into their little 'family.' We studied the philosophies behind Kenpo and Ju-jitsu. We practiced meditations and explored the beauty of these arts. During the time I studied with them, my health improved dramatically. I realized that our focus on mind, body, and spirit was exactly what my body was craving. It responded beautifully.

A few years later, after managing my health relatively well, it crashed again. I experienced stress from a significant trial that seemed to strip away all that I had accomplished. All of the pain came back with even more vengeance. The fatigue was crippling, but this time I had a husband and three children. I was devastated. A few months went by, and I was introduced to essential oils. These ones were effective like I had never seen before. They helped me out of my critical state. As I slowly built up strength, I was reintroduced to tapping. This time it was the Emotional

Freedom Technique. It was a completely new angle at healing that quickly proved effective on my pain and anxiety. I loved the idea of directly impacting my body to not only find relief but profound healing.

This led me to various forms of self-healing modalities. I really struggled with the idea of this at first. The only impression I had of this type of work was that it was voodoo or edgy at best. I soon learned that there's good and bad in this field, and the good was helping me find amazing relief. The first experience I had was with emotional releasing techniques. I mastered that and craved more. I learned how to use the philosophy behind it to remove imbalances all throughout my body. Pretty soon, I was feeling empowered and encouraged that I may have actually found my treasure! A few months went by and I had seen miracles in my own health as well as in my family and friends. I couldn't keep it to myself, could I? This was it. I had finally found the vehicle promised me years earlier through the prayer my father offered. This was a gift directly from heaven.

FAITH

The alternative methods of healing that I experienced acknowledged my body's ability to heal itself if given the right environment and support. The more lessons I learned on my healing journey, the more I realized the power of faith to help the body heal itself. Whether religious or just giving credit to a Divine source of power, many people exercise faith and pray for health, guidance, and even miracles all of the time. Growing up with a strong faith, this angle resonated with me and just made sense to me. I believe it is what led me to the ups and sustained me through the downs. My treasure hunt stemmed from this faith.

Believing in that divine treasure hunt spurred me on to experiment, commit to, and endure several different regimens that promised hope for healing. My faith gave me strength and purpose to keep going through the difficult times. It also opened my mind to be inspired with beautiful truths that helped me manage my health well enough to get married, have children, and hang on until full healing could come. I was still living despite my limitations. I knew that life was important to live as fully as possible, so I lived, dreamed, and worked as hard as I could to live as much of life as I was able to. That determination and faith to keep going contributed powerfully to my eventual healing. The gifts and insights that have come as I endured through it all are invaluable and might just help you to heal as well.

CHAPTER 7

GOLD NUGGETS

"I cannot tell you any spiritual truth that deep within you don't know already. All I can do is remind you of what you have forgotten."

~Eckhart Tolle

During my years of searching, I learned many things. The biggest lessons had to do with shifting out of a victim or pity mentality and stepping into my personal power. I was convinced of my powerlessness. I believed strongly that I couldn't change my life—that no matter what I did, it didn't matter. How wrong I was!

Even though I didn't complain much about my situation, I still held in the back of my mind that I was a victim of this illness, the pain, the limitations—all of it. It took a long time to realize that I was existing under a mindset that could change. These things didn't hold me hostage—I did! I was my own captor. I held myself bound to an invisible and debilitating belief that paralyzed me. Then I woke up; I began to recognize my innate power to change my circumstances and be a proactive contributor to possible solutions. As I did, the more answers I found.

I learned that I could choose how I saw things. I could choose how I attached meaning to things. I learned that I could choose to believe in myself and my potential without worrying so much about the possible disappointment if something didn't work out. I even discovered the power of faith in my life—the reality that we each have a unique and powerful purpose to fulfill. We each matter! I matter. What a paradigm shift! As I adopted these lessons, I grew stronger and more determined that I would indeed eventually be healed.

THE POWER OF CHOICE

The first lesson I learned in overcoming a victim mentality was the power of our minds and our ability to choose. Our choices create our reality. We can choose our attitudes. We can choose how we spend our time. We can choose what we give our attention to. We can choose how we respond to our circumstances. How we respond to events in our lives determines the outcome and our experience, whether we experience growth or digression.

Our perceptions that we adopt really matter. The perspective we choose in any given moment will determine our thoughts, beliefs, and actions. If we focus on the positive side of things, we will see evidence of how they might be beneficial to us. We can see the possible blessings more easily when we are looking for them. Dr. Lissa Rankin shares in her book *Mind Over Medicine* that people with optimistic attitudes are generally better off physically, emotionally, and mentally than those with pessimistic attitudes. Those who are optimistic are often happier, more likely to respond well to disappointment, and live longer lives. Since we can choose, why wouldn't we want to see the glass half-full when it can do us so much good?

While we are choosing our stories, we might as well write ourselves in as one of the strong characters. It's all about perspective, right? Who would consciously choose to write themselves in as victims? In fact, while we're at it, let's write ourselves in as the heroes! I've learned that I'd much rather be the hero of my own story than the victim. It's not a big jump, even if you have been a victim. It is quite reasonable to assume that most people have been or will be victims of one sort or another in their lives. Have you seen a movie or read a book where a character started out great, had a great life and ended up the hero of the story without struggle or disappointment? Of course not; that would be totally anti-climactic. The hero is usually the character that overcomes nearly impossible odds and triumphs in the end. That's powerful! That's inspiring! That's us! We can each be that hero that overcomes our trials, rises to our full potential, and saves the day.

In every moment, we define our experiences. We give meaning to every encounter. Some things are insignificant and thus have less impact. Sometimes we are handed disappointment or even tragedy. We still have the opportunity to define what those experiences will mean to us. The stories we create around those events will affect us positively or negatively for as long as we hold onto them. We can choose to create stories for ourselves that build toward success, meaning, and joy; in fact, we can absorb a feeling or even a persona that builds us up. We can choose to listen to music that lifts us. We can read a book or quote that inspires us. We can even watch a show that fills us with energy.

I remember watching a show where the main character was undeniably brilliant. We watched him work through a problem with genius insight, clever wit, and keen awareness. When we finished the show, I felt smart! My mind was clear and aware. My thoughts traveled through several situations where I displayed my own brilliance. It was such a cool feeling! Another time I watched a show where the hero was brave and determined to conquer his challenges despite overwhelming odds. When the show was over, I was excited about my life and felt empowered to achieve great things.

I realized that we can choose to do this for ourselves at any time. If we're expected to accomplish a certain task that feels daunting, we can play a song that stirs us to move and instills a sense of our ability to fulfill our task. Somehow, it's no longer daunting. We have a new feeling of belief and confidence. I know this because I just finished listening to one of those epic songs in order to feel capable of writing tonight and it helped tremendously.

When we watch that triumphant show, listen to that moving song, read that empowering passage, or even just speak positive and encouraging words to ourselves, we create within us a paradigm that's in alignment with our chosen perspective. We intentionally create a sensation within us for a predetermined purpose—to feel powerful, peaceful, up to the challenge, etc.—that's useful for dealing with our current challenge. It's more than just getting pumped up; it's personifying the particular characteristics of the show's character, the song or the words—being smart, clever, powerful, insightful, determined, inspired, or any other positive frequency or trait. We can choose how we feel, think, and act in remarkable ways.

THE POWER OF BELIEF

The next thing I learned that shifted my perspective out of being a victim was the power of belief. Napoleon Hill said, "Whatever the mind can conceive and believe, it can achieve." We've heard this in several different ways. Henry Ford said, "Whether you think you can, or you think you can't-- you're right." Why not assume the best and see what you can do *without* preconceived limitations? It really isn't better to let doubt rule your life. It's much better to reach for the stars and only catch the moon. It's even better to hope big and be disappointed. Really! As we conquer our minds and constantly choose to see the world in a way that supports our health and success, we can start

31

getting creative.

When we actively choose what we want to believe in, we are in control. We can fill our minds with things that strengthen us and lift us. We can choose to believe that we are strong, capable of great joy, and born into this world to make it a better place. When we allow others to create our beliefs for us, we are subject to their perspectives and their limitations. They don't know what we can become. Don't let them put a lid on your light! We can be intentional about belief in ourselves. We can each choose our own paradigms—ones that are positive, productive, and hopeful.

We can have the desires of our hearts. When we set our hearts on goals and tasks that we want to accomplish, the universe supports us in those worthwhile desires. Opportunities arise and experiences guide us to achieving those things. We can only recognize them when we are open to receiving them. The more we choose to think positive thoughts and believe in our possibilities, the more we access those experiences that we seek.

One of my clients got frustrated when I shared some of these principles with him. He said that he'd heard them before and could never make them work for him. So, what's the difference? Why do these principles work for some people and not for others? In my experience, one of the factors is the level of belief. Did he truly believe that these would work for him? Did he stick with his goals through the whole process? Was he clear about his goals in the first place? If we don't really know what we want, how can we believe in ourselves to get it?

A little later in this book, I'll take you through the process that not only resolved my challenges, but many of my clients' problems as well. You'll see how they build up and help the rubber hit the road. Let me share with you another principle that helped me get closer to discovering the key.

THE POWER OF FAITH

The final key that helped me shift out of victimhood was understanding the incredible power of faith. There are two parts to faith: first, discovering that our lives have a purpose; and second, taking intentional action that creates a new reality.

The first part of faith was remembering clear impressions that I had a purpose to fulfill in my life. Depending upon who we ask, we can find a variety of answers to this question "Why are we here?" Some people have no clue. Others think it's all meaningless and we are the results of a cosmic accident. Well, that's quite hopeless. I'm grateful that I was raised with faith and beliefs that validate my existence, my worth to breathe the air and that I am made for greatness. While I didn't always recognize this as a reality, I do now. I have faith in this principle for everyone on the planet, whether they *choose it* or not. We all have powerful potential. We are not accidents. We are here in this life to learn, grow, and create beautiful things. Simply because we were born, we deserve to live. Accepting that we are valuable and have worth in the world no matter our histories or circumstances can open us up to becoming who we are meant to be.

We each have a unique mission to perform during our lives. We were created to bless this world and help each other along our paths. I know this with every part of me. We are meant to serve the world with our gifts. We are not here by accident; we are here on purpose. We have opportunities ahead of us that we can choose to play full out with or decline participation in. As we learn what our paths look like, what feels good, what we enjoy, and what we're good at, we become more ready to serve in our unique ways. No one else can fulfill our purpose as well as we can.

The second part of the power of faith is action. I didn't recognize what was happening at the time, but as I took intentional action with the purpose of changing my circumstances, I discovered that faith really is a principle of power. And this power could help me change my reality. This kind of faith is applied intention that accesses a power greater than our own.

My faith-filled actions led me to discover the physical and life healing I needed. Through this journey, I overcame my victim mentality, and I began to see clearly. My identity as a victim turned into my identity as a survivor, and then as a *thriver*. I have the power to heal, to thrive, and to help others do the same. These are the lessons that shaped me and prepared me to move forward.

CHAPTER 8

SEEING CLEARLY

*"A man sees in the world
what he carries in his heart."*

~ Goethe

Now that we've uncovered the destructive perception of victim mentality, we can begin seeing clearly where we're going. Not only can we see better where we've been, what we have become because of it, and even where we're going, we can start seeing our worth and our potential. We can choose our own paths and even be the heroes of our lives.

I often see people who are ready, willing and very capable to achieve their goals, but they don't know where to start or how to move forward; they don't have a vision for where they're going. As we work together to help them take responsibility for their choices, build their belief in themselves and their possibilities, and strengthen their faith in their power to make changes in their lives, they can see more clearly what needs to heal so that they can truly move forward. Some need to heal the negative thoughts that keep them down. Others need to understand and apply the power of forgiveness. Most need to learn how to honestly love themselves.

In order to see clearly, we must engage our power to choose. Choosing to limit negative thoughts helps us begin clearing out the junk. Those conversations we have in our heads can be productive or destructive. We can start by recognizing when we're having those conversations. If we can catch them before they get ugly, we're on our way to freedom. Then we can consciously choose what those conversations sound like. Talking nicely to ourselves is super productive; so is talking nicely about others. Refraining from mentally or verbally judging someone helps us feel safer and more valuable because we're not creating an internal reality that's unsafe for people to be themselves or make mistakes.

When we choose to think and feel positive thoughts and emotions, we begin to see clearly. We feel more joy. We can learn to be grateful for the good and bad that happens to us. We're framed to see the lessons better and grow from them. We get to choose how we respond and when we do, we control our emotions and moods. We can choose to be happy! In fact, only *we* can make ourselves happy. No person or thing has the power to do that for us. It's up to us. An amazing thing about it is that the more we choose to be happy, the easier it gets. Eventually, we'll find that it's easy to receive love, love others, and love ourselves too. As we focus on choosing positive thoughts and feelings, we are filled with that light and it's easier to see the good in ourselves, which makes it easier to actually have that beautiful, healthy love for ourselves. Now that's powerful.

To move forward with clarity, we also need to forgive. We need to build up, not tear down. The more we forgive ourselves and others for weaknesses and mistakes, the happier and more peaceful we will be. Seriously, we are all human and do dumb things! When we blow it, let's take care of what we need to, move on and do better next time. Forgiving ourselves and others for their stuff and how it affects us is empowering too. We don't gain anything by holding onto feeling hurt. We can't hurt them nearly as much as we hurt ourselves by staying stuck. It's not only heavy, sad, and frustrating; it literally limits our progression and can make us sick.

As we begin seeing clearly, we recognize the misunderstanding prevalent in society that it's not ok to love ourselves. Many people, especially us women struggle to believe that we can actually experience pure, sweet, healthy love for ourselves. This is not arrogance. It's not selfishness. It's real, it's good, and it's necessary. This kind of love is what helps us take care of our needs. It helps us be kind to ourselves. It helps us not be affected by others' hurtful comments to us. With this kind of love, we protect ourselves from succumbing to bad choices, dangerous habits, and harmful relationships, or experiencing neglect. We make choices that keep us safe, healthy, and truly happy. Additionally, it's only with this kind of pure self-love that we can honestly and fully love others the way they deserve to be loved. We are not concerned about what we can get from others because we are already filling our critical needs. We don't need approval from random people, we don't need acceptance from the in-crowd, and we don't need someone to tell us that we're loveable. We already know we are, and we treat everyone with that same perspective.

I struggled with not seeing clearly for most of my life. It didn't make sense to anyone on the outside, but feeling worthless was very real to me on the inside. I was not loveable. I made stupid mistakes. I had hurt people's feelings. I wasn't worthy of love. Nobody that I can recall told me I was worthless; there was just an accumulation of experiences throughout my life that seemed to prove it to me. I didn't deserve to be happy. I know many of us can relate.

After a while, my choices to see the good in my life, forgive myself and others, and truly begin loving myself changed me. I saw clearly for the first time. I'm not bad; I'm human. Rather than deserve to be miserable, I was created to be happy and am worthy of love. I felt this overwhelming peace and reassurance. I felt compassion for myself. I even began to feel pure, sweet love for myself. It was the most amazing feeling I had ever felt. I realized I could love myself — every simple, flawed, quirky, awkward and mistake-ridden part of me. I'm free!

Since I began seeing clearly, my growth in healthy self-love has been amazing. It's not perfect, but it's been easier to heal. It's been easier to love others unconditionally. It's been transforming and I'm getting better and better at it all the time. The wonderful side effect of it all is that I'm lighter, happier, and freer of self-judgment and judging others than ever before. So, here's the official invitation to choose to recognize your own power, forgive yourself and others—it really is about you moving forward—and set the intention to love yourself the way heaven loves you. You will see your life, your power, and your path more clearly. You're worth all of it!

CHAPTER 9

WE CAN CHANGE
OUR PHYSIOLOGY

"You have the power to heal yourself,
and you need to know that.
We think so often that we are helpless, but we're not.
We always have the power of our minds.
Claim and consciously use your power."

~Louise Hay

As we choose to think about and feel the positive things in our lives, believe in our possibilities, and exert faith or intention to shift our realities, we begin to see our paths more clearly and our bodies and lives begin to change. These three principles—choice, belief, and the power of faith—that helped me get on the path to heal are the same three pieces that prepare people to access self-healing. They will help you later in this book as you begin applying the techniques of *Perfect Healing©*.

The thing that necessarily facilitates self-healing is that the body is designed to heal itself. It can replace itself almost entirely—cells, organs, skin, etc.—in a matter of months. Its ability to heal itself is nothing short of miraculous. Along with that is the built-in ability for us to have an influence over those innate healing functions. We can help soothe a pain, lift a cloud of con fusion, raise our energy, and refresh a heavy mood just by thinking about them!

Science is validating these principles and discovering this inherent power in all of us. Researchers are studying how our choices, thoughts, and feelings affect our physiology. Masaru Emoto, a Japanese author and researcher, articulates, "What we imagine in our minds becomes our world." Evidence continues to mount, supporting the role of the mind in healing. Says Oakley Ray, Professor Emeritus of Psychology, Psychiatry and Pharmacology at Vanderbilt University, "According to the mind-body— or biopsychosocial paradigm—which supersedes the older biomedical model, there is no real division between mind and body because of networks of communication that exist between the brain and neurological, endocrine and immune systems" (Brower, 2006). Scientists are learning how thoughts and feelings create chemical messages that communicate with our cells. These communications tell our cells how to function—positively or negatively. Different scientific disciplines are even working together to understand the effects of light and energy on our biological functions. They are proving that we have innate abilities to facilitate the natural healing functions of our bodies.

We make ourselves sick all the time with negativity and stress. We worry about finances or a child's wellbeing and give ourselves ulcers. We focus on the deterioration of social morality or natural disasters and develop heart disease. Everything is connected. We recognize this, and yet the cycle continues. Negative thoughts, emotions, and energy lead to illness and misery. I think it's time to shift the trends.

All it takes is a belief in your innate influence and some clear intention, and the options for support are nearly endless. With a desire to change your reality, you can see any number of results from simple efforts. What would you most like to resolve in your inner life? Do you have physical challenges? Are you plagued by emotional issues that keep you unhappy? What fears hold you back from really living? What prevents you from enjoying life? You have the power to overcome these obstacles. The power inside of you awaits your command to respond to your needs.

Each word we think or say contributes a certain vibration to our bodies and even those around us. When we think about negative words like "war" or "unworthy," we literally invite their vibrations into us. We begin to feel heavy, sad, or overwhelmed. Maybe our necks even begin to ache. Our bodies respond physiologically to these words. When we choose think about positive words like "peace" or "valuable," we begin to feel their vibrations lift and lighten us. Our physiology responds positively! Say these words to yourself and see how your body responds. Notice how you feel drained or stressed with the negative words and soothed, energized, or empowered with the positive words. These feelings you notice are evidence of literal physical changes within you. We can consciously choose words with particular vibrations to accomplish specific tasks inside of us. We can change our physiology with our thoughts!

The three principles of choice, belief, and faith lead to literal changes in our physiology as well as in our lives as a whole. I've seen the changes in my own life, my family's lives, as well as in the lives of people I work with. We can make things happen that felt impossible before.

What kind of life do you want to create? What legacy do you want to leave? In the end, it's really a matter of the relationships we treasured, the differences we were able to make and who we became during it all. We can own this life, our joys, and our triumphs if we choose to. By the power of the principles we've discussed and the healing modalities we will yet discuss, we can effectively utilize the treasure within us to heal, create joy, and live meaningful lives.

Citation: Brower, V. (2006). Mind—body research moves towards the mainstream. *EMBO Reports*, 7(4): 358—361. doi: 10.1038/sj.embor.7400671

Chapter 10

Messages From The Body

"The body only wants to heal,
it's crying out to heal."

~ Jason Vale

While our bodies are designed to heal and we have the ability to facilitate that healing, we still need to know when and where the body needs help so that we can respond accordingly. There are actually systems in place to help us with this. Every ache, frustration, or symptom of any sort is a message from our bodies. They are smoke signals trying to get our attention. It's easy to be upset by pain or fatigue, but these are simply the body's way of asking for help. Your body is not trying to annoy you or drive you crazy, it is actually communicating with you through the language it's been given. It is our job to listen and respond.

The purpose of these messages is to help us have a better life, become the person we are meant to be, and accomplish the wonderful things we are meant to do! The more in tune with our body and its needs, the quieter the messages. It will whisper first, then speak a bit louder, and finally yell, then throw a tantrum until you finally pay attention and take care of the need. The sooner you hear the messages and take the necessary measures to resolve the concern, the easier it is to fix.

Sometimes we have a random repeating problem. For example, I use muscle response testing to ask what my body or my life needs. I actually rely on it quite heavily. Interestingly, my muscle testing constantly needs to be fixed. It seems like I'm forever resolving obstacles and weaknesses to it working properly. There are things in our bodies that need to be healed that we may not recognize any other way, so the body will find an outlet that we rely on, in order to assure that it will be addressed. Are all the obstacles that continually show up to thwart my muscle testing *really* solely related to it? I doubt it. What makes more sense is that this is an easy outlet for a large amount of chaos to rise to the surface to be addressed. It all needs to come out. Why not have it come out through something that I rely on, that I need to work for me? It's a place where I won't just pass over because I'm tired of working on it. I will always respond to the need and resolve the problem there.

I suppose the best part about my muscle testing being the "smoke signal" is that it's a relatively mild inconvenience compared to the possibilities. It's not debilitating pain (which I've had plenty of!), overwhelming emotions, or challenges with one of my children that I have to work on to remove all that chaos. Don't get me wrong: sometimes it is those things, so I'm grateful when it's just my muscle testing. Therefore, keep an eye out for your repeating outlet. Be grateful for it and all the messages your body communicates to you. Treat it as a blessing that you get to evacuate all that yuck instead of letting it stay put and causing additional problems.

CHAPTER 11

THE TREASURE

"Healing takes courage, and we all have courage, even if we have to dig a little to find it."

~ *Tori Ames*

From principles to application, we move forward in our treasure hunt. In my search for healing, I discovered the priceless treasure of alternative healing modalities. These methods are mind and body practices that focus on the interactions between mind, body, and energy in an effort to enhance physical, mental, and emotional health. Early on I studied several books on the topic and researched two specific modalities. The first, called "tapping," uses energy meridians (like in acupuncture) to shift vibrational reactions and calm emotions. The second, an emotional release technique also works with the energy of our bodies to calm emotions and related physical discomforts. Because of my constant pain and fatigue, I was willing to try anything. Before diving in, however, I studied what makes them work. Once I felt comfortable that these healing modalities were good and effective, and that God had led me to them, I worked hard to apply their techniques.

I started dabbling in the first modality—tapping. I learned quickly that I could feel the shift in my emotions as well as in my pain. I was amazed! I could actually influence how I felt physically and emotionally. Even though I couldn't see the energy moving to help me feel better, the relief was very real. It was remarkable to me. I suddenly felt hope that I could change my health and happiness. With this early success, I was motivated to keep learning and practicing. I became good at it. Three months passed with slow and steady improvement in my health, and then I was introduced to the second method of healing.

This second modality, an emotional release technique felt to me like a step-up. I practiced it and improved my skill over just a few weeks until I was quite confident in its practice. I went back and forth between this and tapping, but I grew to appreciate the speed and ease of the emotional release technique.

After a while, I found that I was, in a way, outgrowing these modalities. My skill was surpassing the techniques. I realized that the hand movements in the modalities were actually unnecessary, that my intention was enough. I learned to ask questions through muscle response testing, which simplified my efforts and helped me see that my skill had amplified beyond either modality.

I continued to expand my understanding by exploring the science behind these and other healing modalities. I learned some amazing things about how our brains work, how our bodies are designed to heal themselves. and that we have more of an influence on our physiology than we realize. I was amazed and excited! *Eureka! Is that what I've been doing this whole time?* People need to know this!

From there, I began distilling down everything that I was learning into the simplest form I could. I realized that all these modalities boiled down to using our intention and desire to facilitate healing. It was all about faith. After months of expanding my knowledge and simplifying it to core principles, I formed the basic structure of my system—the *Perfect Healing©* System. It is beautiful, simple and incredibly effective.

Since its creation, I've used my system and its techniques with dozens of people and seen profound changes in mental, emotional, and physical health, not to mention my own triumph of finally overcoming 18 years of chronic pain, fatigue, and other such misery. I have cried in gratitude more times than I can count. Seeing the same improvements in others' lives was even more exciting! It can work for others, too!

At that point, I knew I needed to share this wonderful work with as many as would listen. I knew there were so many more people who were looking for relief and I wanted them to feel hope and see that they could heal too!

Keep reading and you'll learn for yourself the beautiful simplicity of this wonderful work. I've labored through everything, worked through the stages from complicated to simple and around again. It is powerful, yet accessible, so you don't have to work so hard. You, too, will be able to achieve your dreams. I'm so excited for you!

Chapter 12

Your *Perfect* Journey

"Hardships often prepare ordinary people
for an extraordinary destiny."

~ *C.S. Lewis*

We've talked about the principles behind affecting our physiology. This won't be completely useful to you until we apply them to your life. You may not believe this, but your journey is perfect. By perfect, I'm referring to how each of our journeys to health, success, and happiness is perfect. The experiences we have and lessons we learn are tailored to our perfect growth. Yes, they can be difficult and even debilitating at times, but they are what we need to become our best selves. Through my personal development and healing system, I have been able to overcome some extremely difficult challenges—things that plagued me for years—chronic illnesses, self-criticism, and trauma. As I've looked back over these years and the many lessons I've learned, I am able to see how those challenges have been perfect for my growth and healing. They have nurtured me along a path toward wholeness and joy. They have led me to live a *life above the line.*

I know that in the midst of trials the journey doesn't look perfect. Along my path to healing, I remember searching for relief, answers, and sometimes someone to blame. I'll admit it, it wasn't right, but that's what I was doing. I believe I was doing this because the suffering felt so oppressive and overwhelming. Thank heaven for hindsight. Lessons seem to become clearer after the trial is over.

As I recognized the principles of choice, belief, and faith, my vision became clear. I forgave myself. I chose to focus on solutions instead of the problems. Again, hindsight is great. The more aware I've become of what's really going on in my body and my life, the more conscious I am of learning the lessons I need *during* the trial instead of months or years later. I'm learning to ask myself how my challenges are perfect for me and I love what I've found. The new perspective and understanding I receive help make the challenge more manageable. I'm not fighting against my growth as perhaps I once did. I embrace the lessons and the growth with gratitude.

What I'm finding now is that I am less reactive to challenges. I don't get so upset or ask "Why me?" I don't go looking for someone to blame. I am more patient and peaceful. I trust the process of life. I trust that there's a plan for me and my life and that my challenges are helping me grow in ways that I couldn't have imagined before. I'm more confident and sure about the direction my life is taking. I am even excited about my life path, whereas before I felt a bit lost and anxious about what my future held. I'm no longer afraid. I can handle anything that comes my way.

CHAPTER 13

MIND OVER MATTER

*"It all begins and ends in your mind.
What you give power to, has power over you,
if you allow it."*

~ *Leon Brown*

As we get into responding to these messages from our bodies, it really is a simple and beautiful dance we are allowed to participate in. We'll get to the techniques for responding in just a bit, but first I'll give you an idea of what's really going on as we facilitate the healing of our bodies and our lives.

Let's explore some science to illustrate why we don't have to have an intuitive gift, be some kind of "mystic," or meditate in the Himalayas for thirty years to unlock the mysteries of what our minds and bodies can do. In fact, research during the last couple of decades is showing that this work isn't "mystical" at all. On the contrary, it's straightforward, intellectually sound, and rather simple to explain through scientific inquiry.

Now, I hesitate just a little about diving into the scientific side, because there's so much available to study that it would be easy to get lost in the research and forget what this work is all about, which is simply to help us heal. As Dr. Joe Dispenza, a thought leader in neuroscience, neuroplasticity, and the like said at a recent conference: "We should never wait for science to give us permission to do the uncommon."

In today's world of western medicine and big pharma, this type of work fits in the "uncommon" category, but I know firsthand—from my own experiences and those of dozens of others—that it works, and works well.

That being said, I'm going to take some of the mystery out of this work so we can see and understand what's going on in the healing process and how our bodies operate.

First, let's consider some common phenomena and understandings. We all know—or at least we can all identify with the reality—that we can literally affect our physiology with thoughts, emotions. and intentions. They resonate through the body with either healing or destructive messages. Happy messages create order and proper function while negative ones create chaos and imbalance.

For example, when people worry, their stomachs may become upset and experience butterflies or nausea. Or if a person even thinks about going up on a stage and addressing a few hundred people, it can make their stomach drop. Nobody punched them in the stomach and they didn't go over a hill on a roller coaster, but they felt it!

Or maybe a parent hears a crash in the other room where their kids are playing. There's that "zap" that goes throughout their body. No one shocked them with electricity and yet they felt something very much like it. It seemed very real, yet they merely imagined a frightful scenario.

Have you ever really thought about why someone's face turns red when they are embarrassed? It's just an emotion and yet the physiological response can be seen.

When we are excited about a project or opportunity, we often feel better emotionally and physically. We have certainly seen this in children. They have a meltdown for one reason or another, then someone offers up a fun activity to engage in and —voila— they are suddenly better and ready to play. I experienced this for myself during my years of chronic illness. When I had a meaningful project to focus on, I seemed to draw energy from out of nowhere. I had stamina and motivation, whereas I hardly moved around normally. I could live more fully when I was excited about something.

CHAPTER 14

MORE THAN JUST
POSITIVE THINKING

"Whatever you can do, or dream you can, begin it.
Boldness has genius, power and magic in it."

~ *Goethe*

But what goes on in the body to make all this happen? In the past few years some brilliant doctors and scientists have made wonderful strides in helping us understand how this really works. In their experiences, research, and studies, they discovered exactly how chemicals, vibrations, and energies deliver instructions throughout our bodies and produce predictable results.

A traditionally trained physician, Dr. Lissa Rankin teaches in her book *Mind Over Medicine* how our beliefs and attitudes affect our physical reality. Negativity can lead to illness: if a person believes that they'll get sick, they likely will. She references a study where hospitalized patients were given a placebo medication made up of sugar water and told that they may experience some side effects. They were told that it could make them throw up and 80% of them did!

On the other hand, positive beliefs and perspectives can lead to wellness. Dr. Rankin shares research that shows how optimistic people are healthier. There are fewer rates of heart disease, they recover better after surgery, and they tend to live longer.

Hope is a powerful healer. People who believe they can overcome their struggles are more likely to be healthy or recover from illness. Feeling hopeful can help reduce stress responses and strengthen our immune system. People with a positive sense of wellbeing are more resistant to stress and the many stress-related health issues.

Dr. Rankin also tells of the Spontaneous Remission Project, which is a database containing about 3,500 references of unexplainable disease remissions and miraculous healings. "A man's brain aneurysm disappeared." "A woman with thyroid disease experienced a spontaneous cure." Western medicine scratches its head when things like this happen. But the research is there and it's powerful.

QUANTUM PHYSICS

The Quantum Physics world understands how our minds affect our realities. Thankfully, we don't have to be quantum physicists to get this next part; it is helpful, however to know about some of what they're learning. Scientists are discovering the connections between our thoughts and our realities. They are studying the smallest particles we know of and watching them react to simple observation. They're studying subtle energy and how it affects our physiology. In research, they're learning that the intentions of our minds can affect how our genes are expressed, thus affecting our health. They're discovering that we have creative powers—we just need to be conscious of what we're creating.

NEUROSCIENCE

Neuroscience is also teaching us about neuroplasticity and how the once held belief that our brains cannot change is gone. Neuroplasticity helps us understand that we can reprogram our brain and its neural pathways. This affects our behaviors, our capacities and our mental health. This brings new hope for many who thought there was no way to improve their conditions.

PSYCHONEUROIMMUNOLOGY

Candace Pert, a Ph.D. in Psychoneuroimmunology, tells us similar principles in her book *Molecules of Emotion*. She explains the biochemical link between the mind and the body through emotions and "messenger molecules." In fact, she says, "It is the emotions, I have come to see, that link mind and body." This was so validating! It showed me how I survived all those years of pain, fatigue and other yuck. I was on a treasure hunt for what would get me well, and that hope and optimism carried me through.

Dr. Pert even talks about how our physical movements and positions can affect our emotions. You can try it! Roll your shoulders forward, hang your head, and lean on one leg. It feels weak, heavy and discouraging, doesn't it? Now, stand up tall, put your hands on your hips, shoulders back and your chin up, and smile — you know, like a superhero. Doesn't that feel amazing! If a person stands like that for 2 minutes before they interview for a job or just walk into a room, it creates an actual energetic shift.

EPIGENETICS

Bruce Lipton is a renowned scientist in the field of epigenetics. He teaches us in his book *Biology of Belief* how our thoughts and emotions affect how our cells function; how our DNA is expressed. No longer is genetic determinism king. Our genes do not determine how our lives play out; they are only blueprints. *We* determine how they manifest. We are not simply subject to the health or lack thereof that our parents and grandparents experienced. As we choose more positive environments externally and internally, we can help direct our cells to function in a healthier way, in turn, giving us an experience of better health. He says the chemistry of belief is that our brain sends the messages between our environment and our cells.

So basically, something happens to us and our brain interprets what happens with thoughts and emotions and then proceeds to communicate with our cells to tell them how to respond.

Our minds are programmed through inherited genetics or imprinted through life experiences to respond in a certain way. Remember when we talked about getting up in front of an audience? As we enter that situation, the programs that we run on interpret our involvement. The programming responds with a thought of "Oh no" or "Get me out of here" and sends that message to corresponding receptors that trigger a stress response of nausea, dizziness, or panic. Suddenly we feel sick, ready to pass out, or simply have those classic butterflies in the stomach.

We can change that programming. We are in control. We have the power to choose. Dr. Lipton says there are four ways to reprogram those responses.

- Hypnosis — using subliminal messages
- Repetition — practicing on a regular basis for a long time
- Shock — something traumatic can change our programming quickly (not the most desirable option!)
- Energy Psychology — super-learning, belief-changing modalities

This is a new frontier. I invite you to accept the powerful truth that you have incredible influence over your physical, mental, and emotional health. You can help yourself heal. The techniques you will learn in this book are super-learning and belief-changing methods. Learn them and adopt them into your life.

What would you create for yourself with these kinds of tools? You can create a joyful and meaningful reality!

CHAPTER 15

THE POWER OF INTENTION

"Everybody in the world is seeking happiness —
and there is one sure way to find it.
That is by controlling your thoughts.
Happiness doesn't depend on outward conditions.
It depends on inner conditions."

~*Dale Carnegie*

How do we actually help our bodies heal? How do we activate the wonderful things science has shown us so that we can heal ourselves? You may be thinking that you've hoped for healing or relief of some sort before, maybe even focused serious effort on it, and it didn't come. Trust me, you have the power inside of you. You may have just never used this ability in this way before. It all boils down to your intention. That's right — your focused thought.

Intention is defined by Dictionary.com as "an act or instance of determining mentally upon some action or result; purpose or attitude toward the effect of one's actions or conduct." For me, in this context, it is more like a power that is harnessed by combining the vibrational and energetic levels of our bodies. In other words, as we focus our beliefs, thoughts, emotions, and energy toward a particular result we activate intention. This intention has the power to change the chemistry of our bodies, infuse us with energy, and help our bodies heal themselves.

Grasping the concept that the mind has influence over the physiology of our bodies may be a stretch for some people. That's ok. This healing power is already within us and it's something we use all the time. Some have developed it more than others, but we all access this power to some extent—whether we realize it or not.

We can see where we're at and what else is possible through the lens of a familiar structure: levels of schooling. We learn line upon line with most things in life, so why should understanding how to influence our physiology be any different? Let's start with the basics, so back to grade school!

ELEMENTARY LEVEL — REACTIVE

This is the baseline—the most basic and natural level of human cognitive activity: reaction. At this level we gain an understanding that thinking and entertaining bad or negative thoughts can lead to bad things. Since we don't want bad things to happen, we usually listen to that advice to avoid or ignore those kinds of thoughts. We learn to be aware of our thoughts so we can keep bad thoughts out.

Early on, those thoughts can tell us to be grumpy at our siblings or scare us into believing that there are monsters under our beds. Later on, they can tell us that we're dumb, worthless, or don't belong. They can be triggered by stories we hear, experiences we have, or things we see.

We can be taught to react to negative thoughts positively by recognizing them and then dismissing them. We try to replace the thoughts, too, by thinking of something cheerful, singing a happy song, or by discerning the truth from the error in the thought. In these efforts we are taking baby steps to gain control of our minds.

MIDDLE SCHOOL LEVEL — REACTIVE TO PROACTIVE

At the next level, we become more proactive than reactive. We're not leaving our life experience up to others quite so much. Here, we choose to think positive thoughts.

If we are faced with something daunting, we can choose to respond to the situation by preparing ourselves as well as possible. Some examples of these might be getting ready to go on stage to perform, knowing there's a test at school that day, or facing up to a mistake we've made. Whatever the situation, we don't settle for being afraid or nervous, or leaving things up to chance. We choose to proactively engage a positive mindset to manage our emotions.

Instead of just reacting to negativity or a difficult situation when it happens, we decide to think ahead of time how we will respond, look for the best in the scenario or focus on keeping ourselves clear-headed and calm. We consciously choose to think positive thoughts to prepare and to build ourselves up. We are proactive in directing our minds to survive a challenge.

SECONDARY SCHOOL LEVEL —PROACTIVE TO CREATING

In this level, we enter creation mode. We are not just reacting or even simply setting ourselves up to succeed. We are actually creating our success. Here, we use the power of our thoughts to lift our emotions.

It's about choice. We can choose our reality. If we sense the tendency to see the hard things in life, feel overwhelmed or feel bad about ourselves, we can change this with the power of our thoughts. We can choose our attitudes and how we experience life. As my father always told me, "Your attitude determines your altitude." It really is up to us how we feel.

We have filters in us that interpret our life experiences and essentially tell us how we think and feel about what happened.

As we recognize the value of intentional, positive thinking, we can choose to use its influence to help us improve the quality of these filters. We can have greater and greater control over our minds *and* our emotions. We discover that we can choose to be happy, peaceful, grateful, etc.

UNIVERSITY LEVEL — CREATING TO REORGANIZING

At this level, we continue in creation mode as we facilitate overall health. We begin using the power of our thoughts intentionally to help heal our bodies and minds. We can meditate on healing words or visualizations to feel lasting peace after a disappointment, feel relief from a headache, or heal more quickly from an illness.

This is where science is so validating. As discussed in chapter thirteen, disciplines such as Epigenetics, Quantum Physics, and Psychoneuroimmunology teach us how our thoughts and emotions literally affect our physiology. We can change the elements inside of us and take them from chaotic to organized, from destructive to healing. Our bodies are designed to heal themselves and we have the power to help in that process. It only makes sense!

We see it all the time and are very familiar with the principle. We may just not recognize it for what it is. For example, if we can feel stress or even just think stressful thoughts and produce a stomachache, then why can't we think positive, healing thoughts and soothe the stomachache? We *can*! We can strengthen our digestive system to process a meal better or our nervous system to manage our stress better. We can help ourselves heal from pretty much anything.

But wait, there's even more.

MASTER'S LEVEL

At the master level, we go beyond ourselves. We use the innate power of our thoughts and intentions to help others' bodies, minds and hearts heal. Yes, really! We do it to one extent or another already without even knowing it.

What you may or may not know is that we all radiate energy. People feel that energy when we walk into a room. Have you ever just sensed how someone is feeling? They walk into the room and you can sense the vibe they're giving off. That feeling can be happy and attractive or negative and repelling. For the most part we are unaware of the energy we give off. That's not always a good thing.

We get to choose to be responsible for the energy we radiate. We can contribute positivity to an environment. We can even focus positive energy toward someone. If you're religious, this is similar to praying for someone. For parents, we often direct positive energy toward our children—soothing a crying baby or comforting an injured child. We send them love and real, healing energy. In the same vein, it's valuable to be aware of negative energy we may send our children. They can feel that too.

DOCTORAL LEVEL

The doctoral level is where we have gained significant control over our minds and our external environment. This is the full expression of the power of faith. There are stories in history that show this kind of power. If necessary, we can move mountains, part seas, heal instantaneously, and so forth. Perhaps someday we can rise to this level.

The same power that makes all of this possible also makes possible each of the other levels. This level utilizes this power to its full potential, but it is available to us in degrees at each level of progression.

For us, in this book, we're choosing to take charge where we can. We're accepting responsibility for our thoughts and emotions. We're choosing to exercise our power to heal. We're starting a beautiful process to create the healthy and bright lives we truly desire.

CHAPTER 16

FIVE AREAS OF HEALING

"For every effect there is a root cause. Find and address the cause rather than try to fix the effect, as there is no end to the latter."

~ *Celestine Chua*

Up to this point, we've been focusing on the principles of living a *life above the line.* Now we're going where the rubber hits the road, where all the science, belief, and intention can really make a difference in our lives. There are five areas in which the body needs to be healed. These areas are physical, functional, negative external influences, vibrational, and generational. In the *Perfect Healing©* System, we acknowledge and support each of these areas. This is what facilitates comprehensive healing. We heal every part of the issue.

Health problems and other challenges can be quite complex. A pain lingering in our right wrist might be from a childhood injury, overuse at work, or even stress regarding a totally unrelated aspect of our lives. It may also be a combination of all three. This is why a simple pill can often be ineffective at solving the problem. It may temporarily soothe the discomfort, but it likely won't heal the issue. It seems that true healing is a notion of the past.

The typical modern answer to our complex mental, emo

tional, and physical issues is medication. An analysis of symptoms and easing them is the focus, and the goal, survival. How many conversations do we have with medical professionals that really try to dig down and discover the root causes or all the contributors to the problem? But that right there is a big part of the problem: we don't often know how to find and treat all the root causes. It's like trying to keep a ship from sinking by bailing water with a pail. Unless the source (or sources) of the problem—the hole—is both discovered and taken care of, water will keep spilling in. You may be able to keep up with it and even make some headway; but unless the source is found and attended to, your strength will soon become exhausted and it will appear that all your hard work was for nothing—the ship is sinking anyway. Likewise, addressing the root causes is the only path to true healing. But true healing seems so often to be out of reach.

So there we have it. From our youth we are trained to believe that life is just meant for getting by. We struggle through life's challenges and injustices, squash them down when we don't have any more time, energy, or resources to dwell on them, and then move on. But is that really what we're meant to do? Are we really meant to just get by in life or merely survive?

Obviously, since you're reading this book, you feel like I do: we are meant for much more. We are meant to live with joy. We are meant to thrive! We've addressed how we each have a unique purpose to fulfill in life. That can be difficult when we're miserable with health challenges, negative thoughts running through our heads, and feelings of powerlessness against all that plagues our lives. We've been told it's impossible to get through our obstacles because there's nothing the doctor can do for us. Or we're told that it's just in our heads, or that we just need to get over it. Well, none of that set well with me. Inside, I knew there was a way—I just had to figure it out. And here we are.

When we talk about healing, we need to approach every area

that pulls us below the line. We need to have tools to support our bodies and lives to help us actually heal. That requires not only the physical healing for damage in our bodies, but also strengthening the systems and functions that run our bodies. We also need to remove negative influences around us as well as releasing the ones inside of us. We need to be able to restore our deep inner programming to what it was intended to become—pure and healthy!

So, this is where we begin. We'll learn the steps to resolve each of these areas of influence over our physical, mental, emotional, and overall life health. No longer will we leave potential healing on the table. We can understand and learn from all the problems that we face and know clearly how to resolve them.

* * *

The *Perfect Healing©* System teaches about five words that correspond to each of the five areas of the body that need support for comprehensive healing. These words are HEAL, ADDRESS/STRENGTHEN, REMOVE, RELEASE, and RESTORE and we'll review them in depth over the next few chapters.

These words don't have magic in themselves, as it's our intention that gives them the power to create powerful shifts in our lives and bodies. But with these five words, we can experience true healing—the kind of healing that frees us from our burdens, not just covers them up and this really is just the beginning. We'll continue to gain deeper understanding and build our skills into higher levels of healing and living life.

CHAPTER 17

HEAL

"Healing comes when we choose to walk away from darkness and move towards a brighter light."

~ *Dieter F. Uchtdorf*

For *Perfect Healing©*, there are five primary words. We'll begin with the word HEAL. This step focuses on the physical area of the body. There are times when it is obvious that the body needs physical healing. When we use the word HEAL in the *Perfect Healing©* technique, we ask the body to fix physical damage. Whatever is infected, torn, misaligned, or toxic responds to this request. If there's something broken, scratched, or injured, focusing on the word HEAL invites the body to begin correcting the problem, and it will literally alter the physical elements to align with the body's natural structure and inherent design.

There is a simple yet profound truth we must remember: our bodies are designed to heal themselves. That's right; medications don't heal us, doctors don't heal us, herbs don't heal us, and so on. Each person or remedy on our health team plays a similar role in that they facilitate the body's efforts to heal itself. They can help remove things that don't belong. They can boost our body's functions and protect the structures of the body. But they are not responsible for *healing* the body.

Let's get specific here. We're talking about structures of the body such as organs, glands, fluids, bones, muscles, nerves, teeth, hair, skin, DNA—all those parts of your body that you can see, touch, examine, x-ray, or photograph with a cool machine. Each of these structures has programming built in to help them regenerate when damaged or renew when worn out.

Sometimes our innate healing programs can get off-track. Strained overall health can weaken the body's natural healing mechanisms. Chronic stress can turn these mechanisms off as well. Negative thoughts and beliefs can take us off the health side of the cycle and put us on the illness side. Inherited tendencies can also inhibit normal healing.

Each of these things can be resolved with the simple methods you are learning in this course. Using these techniques gets the body's natural healing back on track. Calming stress can turn the automatic healing systems back on. We can remove obstacles to the body healing itself. Then, the body can resume healing in its natural course.

We can use the word HEAL for a wide variety of issues. Here are a couple of examples that show the scope of this word in the technique:

My middle son injured his leg once. He was having fun on the playground at school when he slipped and cut the front of his shin. It was significant enough to earn him a trip to the doctor and 7 stitches. This incident provided us an opportunity to use HEAL. There was obvious tissue damage and its resulting pain. Notice the word HEAL doesn't take the place of the stitches, but what it did do is help the body respond to the injury and the treatment to its full capacity.

Another example would be lung damage from smoking. Say someone has smoked for several years and has some issues with their breathing caused by this lung damage. Ideally the first course of action is that the individual can stop smoking and turn off the faucet of destruction to the body. The word HEAL can facilitate the repair of damaged tissue in the lungs as well as other parts of the body that sustained harm.

So, quite simply the word HEAL helps fix physical damage in the body.

CHAPTER 18

ADDRESS/STRENGTHEN

"Sometimes you don't realize your own strength until you come face to face with your greatest weakness."

~ *Quotesforbros.com*

The next area of healing uses the word ADDRESS or STRENGTHEN. With these words we're asking the body to improve a function or system. For example, we may want to invite strength into our immune or digestive systems so that these can work properly again if they've been weakened by an illness or a poor choice of food for dinner.

Basically, this step facilitates healing by strengthening a system when it is overloaded or stressed in some way. The concept is that if such and such system were functioning better, it would be able to resolve this concern on its own.

To help you better understand what's happening here, our mental efforts help direct the flow of energy in our bodies. Depending on the culture you're familiar with, energy may be the most comfortable term. If you love India, then prana will resonate with you. If you're a fan of East Asian cultures, then you might like to use the term qi. If you're religious, then you can call it spirit.

Whatever you call it, it's the essence that gives life to our bodies—it's what makes us work! By intending support for the body systems that are needing help, you direct energy there and

70

give it a little boost to help it figure out the problem and begin working to resolve it.

To expand on the food choice example, say you go out to dinner—one of those all-you-can-eat places—and you stuff yourself because, well, the food is great and you enjoy a bargain. The downside to this scenario is that you may feel the repercussions of overindulging. Most of us are guilty of this at times, especially around the holidays. The words ADDRESS or STRENGTHEN can give your digestive system some extra help to work through all that food a little better.

Another place these words are helpful is for the nervous system. Stress is a plague in society today and it can really take a toll on all our systems, particularly the nervous system. This can cause someone to feel fatigued and generally on edge. Their fight-or-flight stress-response mechanisms are strained and running overtime, which is emotionally, mentally, and physically draining. Using ADDRESS or STRENGTHEN can give much-needed support to the functioning of this taxed system and help us start feeling more peaceful, energized, and clear-headed.

CHAPTER 19

REMOVE

*"Strength doesn't come from what you can do.
It comes from overcoming the things
you once thought you couldn't."*

~ *Rikki Rogers*

The word REMOVE eliminates negative external influences. I like to explain it this way: You know those little shoulder angels, one is red with a pitchfork and the other is white with a halo? This step removes the little red bad guy and his negative influence.

You may or may not be aware that these bad guys exist. Let me assure you, they are real and their influence is felt physically, mentally, emotionally, and energetically. These bad guys can initiate physical illness in any form: injury, headaches, disease...anything! They can trigger confusion, difficulty focusing, negative and even dangerous thoughts, mental illness, and more. These bad guys can stir up feelings of worthlessness, depression, or anxiety. They can convince you to feel alone, abandoned, or that your case is hopeless.

DON'T LISTEN TO THEM!

The word REMOVE may seem simple and weak in the face of these influences, but trust me, it works. This tool is simple yet effective and you can make it even stronger by adding a few things to your efforts. If you are a person of faith, remember to pray for protection daily. If you like essential oils or supplements, there are some great ones out there that are supportive to these efforts. Your aura is truly like a shield of light. We will learn more ways to help you fortify this protection. In the meantime, you can use the word ADDRESS or STRENGTHEN that I just taught you to help with this.

I realize that the concept of these bad guys and their influence may be foreign to you, or it may be weird to actually talk about this, but I wouldn't bring it up if it wasn't important. Please take this seriously. If they are exerting influence on your life and you begin using the word REMOVE to help yourself, you *will* notice a change.

Also, don't be afraid of choosing to believe in this—ignorance really is not bliss! You can eliminate any fear or anxiety you feel regarding this topic with these techniques and shift into gratitude that you have a tool to help you fight the battles that arise. Try this and you'll be surprised; it's worth it.

This is so important that here's a little bonus for you. Each morning, evening, and however many times during the day you feel like it, say "Boundaries Up." I like preventative measures and this is a good one here. This will help REMOVE any bad guys hanging around and strengthen the protective layers around you, giving you a head start.

I had a profound experience with a student of mine on this subject. While working together, she began making great strides to improve her health and her life. She had been struggling with a number of physical and emotional issues for quite a while, but anxiety and some related physical symptoms were the hardest around this time. She had made so much progress that she was feeling more and more confident in her abilities to tackle whatever came up. Well, one day she went out to run some errands and suddenly the anxiety hit like a freight train. She didn't even feel so much of the emotion of it, just mostly the symptoms of the anxiety. It was weird, but real and debilitating. She texted me for help to figure out what was going on and why it seemed more difficult to calm down than other times. We quickly realized it was them. It became very clear that these bad guys were basically declaring war on her and her powerful goals. We worked on things until she felt better, but it made us that much more determined to beat them.

Simply put, the bad guys are real and they don't like us. They exert great efforts trying to make us sick, afraid to improve our lives, and especially to stop us any way they can from being happy and helping others to be happy. REMOVING them and their influence from your life is a powerful step forward to living a happy, healthy, and truly meaningful life. And remember, Boundaries Up!

Chapter 20

Release

*"Make sure your worst enemy doesn't
live between your two ears."*

~Laird Hamilton

The word RELEASE frees up negative emotions, thoughts, and beliefs that have become stuck in us. They are vibrations that if not taken care of can create emotional, mental, and physical illness. RELEASING them allows the body to function the way it's intended to without debilitating obstacles. With these emotions gone, pain can dissipate, feelings can brighten, and we are freer to think positive thoughts and begin programming new, productive beliefs.

As we learned earlier, thoughts and emotions that are driven by beliefs or programming have scientifically proven effects on our physiology. The word RELEASE, then, becomes extremely important as we work to find relief to all sorts of problems. We can interrupt the cycle between the environment and our cells. We can change our reactions to an event, shift how we think or feel about something or someone. We can reprogram a belief that causes us to react in a destructive way. We can create a more productive and healthy cycle of reactions that actually help us to be more of who we really are and respond consciously and positively to any situation.

Society on the whole hasn't really found a way to teach us how to process emotions and experience them in a healthy, productive way. We're instead taught to ignore, brush aside, or even squash down feelings that are anything but happy. Ironically, we also learn to entertain negative stories that play in our heads, creating terrible scenarios that make us feel worse and worse. This is what we want to get away from—we want to change these destructive habits and become a society of healthy, well-balanced individuals.

The world seems to be getting a bit crazier as time goes on and I believe that those of us who can control our emotions and the stories that we tell ourselves—those inner conversations we hold with ourselves—the more in control we will be of our environment. We will be able to experience peace amid turmoil. We will be able to think clearly and even help those around us who are struggling. Our bodies will be less subject to illness, stress, disease, and other debilitating influences. So much of this can be helped just by using the word RELEASE in this simple, yet profound technique that you will learn.

The word RELEASE is here to help us eliminate the harmful emotions, thoughts, and beliefs that are already programmed inside of us, but they can also help us process things that come at us now. When you feel an uncomfortable emotion during a difficult experience, instead of squashing it only to deal with it later as a headache or indigestion, allow yourself to feel it. Honor it and give it space to flow and move through you. If you feel it and allow it to play out, it will leave. You can even use RELEASE to help you through it in the moment, as it can facilitate healthy processing of current feelings so they don't get stuck!

One of my students' daughters was getting ready for school one morning, but she had a stomachache that was really getting the best of her. She was worried about something and didn't want to go to school. Her mother sat down with her and together, they used RELEASE. She was only 8, but she knew how to think about her stomachache and say RELEASE. They worked on the discomfort together for just a few minutes, and then suddenly she hopped up and finished getting ready for school as if nothing had happened! She was happy and ready for the day.

Another student told me how a painful, discouraging memory from 20 years ago was troubling him while winding down for the night. It was something that had surfaced before, but this time he couldn't get rid of the thought or the strong negative emotions that came with it. By using RELEASE, the agony of the memory began to melt away. After just a few seconds, the memory was still there, but the pain of it was gone. I checked in with him a few months later to see how he was doing with that issue. He happily reported that it just doesn't bother him anymore. The emotional pain is gone.

My husband is a golf enthusiast. He loves to play a round of golf, watch a golf event, or just practice in the back yard. Lately, we've been using these words, including RELEASE, to help him in his golf game. There's a lot that goes into a good round of golf and we're helping him clear away all the obstacles to him playing his best. One of the challenges is moving on to the next hole when he "bogied" the last one. Using RELEASE has been great to calm those frustrations, disappointments, and feelings of discouragement in between holes. It's been great to watch him ground himself again and be able to focus on improving his game and not letting emotions paralyze his progress. Now he helps others with the knowledge and experience he has gained.

As you can see, RELEASE helps with anything you could imagine!

CHAPTER 21

RESTORE

"In every adult there lurks a child—an eternal child, something that is always becoming, is never completed, and calls for unceasing care, attention, and education. That is the part of the personality which wants to develop and become whole."

~ *Carl Jung*

I believe that we were originally created in perfection. The word RESTORE helps us return to that original design. This original, perfect programming gave way to inherited physical, mental, emotional, and other traits from our parents and ancestors when we were conceived. We're familiar with the physical manifestations of this—for instance, you have your mom's eyes or your dad's feet. We each inherit a mixture of DNA from our parents—about 50% from each one. They also gained a similarly mixed DNA inheritance from their parents, and that is the larger DNA pool that we drew from. Our DNA mixture is unique to us, but its specific components are thousands of years old. I have found that we also have an energetic inheritance—energetic genetics, if you will—that is passed on similarly. We inherit elements of the cognitive, emotional, and energetic traits of our ancestors. These are programmed into our overall DNA to make us who we are today. But some of these inherited programs are less than ideal. When we use the word RESTORE, we are removing those imperfect inheritances and RESTORING ourselves back to our perfect programming.

This word is especially effective when you recognize a family pattern, such as headaches, financial propensities, emotional, or behavioral tendencies. RESTORE helps with what is familiarly known as generational healing. As we learned from Bruce Lipton's *Biology of Belief* regarding epigenetics, our futures are not determined solely by our DNA. We do get to influence how those blueprints are read and manifest. We are not powerless victims to what we were given when we were conceived.

RESTORE is also effective against things that become imprinted or conditioned in us over the course of our lives. Sometimes we experience things strongly enough or often enough that they get in and change our DNA without our knowing or wanting them to. This creates a situation where the word RELEASE is not sufficient to resolve these overwhelming feelings or thoughts, because they have actually changed our core programming. So, RESTORE reprograms these imprinted patterns just as though they were inherited ones.

The need for RESTORE can show up as a tendency for depression that you saw in or heard in stories about a grandparent that may have been passed down to you. RESTORE is also useful in situations where you inherited a pattern of headaches, migraines or some other physical weakness. In the situation of imprinting, you may have learned a behavior of impatience from another long-term acquaintance — a friend, babysitter or mentor of some sort — and you later see it in your own tendencies.

One of my students has a family pattern of depression. These are beautiful people with a difficult obstacle to living a happy life. This student recognized the tendency in himself, especially regarding a difficult experience from his past. He realized, as he looked over his life, just how much this tendency toward depression had impacted him. We used many of the words to help him through these challenges, and especially RESTORE with regard to his inherited patterns. He is no longer plagued by feelings of powerlessness when he feels sad or disappointed. Depression doesn't rule his life like it once did. He now manages his emotions with these tools.

Remember what I shared earlier about my son and his injured leg that needed stitches? We not only used the word HEAL on him to help repair the injured tissue, but we used all five of these words. We used STRENGTHEN to help his immune system function perfectly to fight off infection. We used REMOVE to fight off the negative thoughts that were trying to creep in from the "bad guys." We used RELEASE to help him process the emotions of the trauma itself, as well as prevent any beliefs from sticking that could cause him to limit himself in the future. We also used RESTORE to help the inherited patterns of physical and emotional healing return back to where they needed to be in order for him to heal properly and completely. From these efforts he has healed beautifully, both physically and emotionally!

These 5 words of HEAL, ADDRESS or STRENGTHEN, REMOVE, RELEASE and RESTORE may seem simple, but they are powerful enough to make dramatic changes in your health, happiness, and success. They are sufficient to facilitate focus and create clear intentions to direct healing in your body and your life. These are the steps to resolve each of the areas of influence over our physical, mental, emotional, and overall life health. We are meant to live with joy! We are meant to thrive!

Chapter 22

Perfect Healing© Technique

"What if you were willing to step into your greatness,
not greatness of ego, but greatness of a
realization of the power of choice that you've been
given by your Creator? The greatness of who you are
capable of being when you are acting from your high-
est self. The greatness that you know lives within you
and it just needs to be unbound again."

~ Brendon Burchard

Now that you've learned the basic principles and words of *Perfect Healing©* that can help you live your *life above the line*, you're ready to learn how to put them into practice. In this chapter, you'll learn the life-enhancing techniques I've been talking so much about.

Since we can employ our minds to help us heal, let's get familiar with some important keys for making it work well.

First, we must *choose* to make a change. We must be willing to let go of what is holding us back. Sometimes this is easier said than done, but it is critical for success. The more specific we get about what we want to change, the clearer our results will be. So, just thinking "I want to feel better" isn't as effective as thinking "I want to feel happier or more peaceful" or "I want to feel that I am enough" or "I want this pain to go away." What answers are you searching for? What pain, frustration, worry, or negativity do you want relief from? That's what you want to *choose* to let go of and focus your efforts on.

Second, we must *believe* it's possible to change and improve our realities. We've discussed how our bodies and our lives are designed to heal and that science even validates that we can influence that process. Also, choosing our thoughts here is important as they can build our *belief* in change and our ability to create that change or they can tear down that *belief* and prevent our efforts from taking effect. So, choose to *believe* in the possibilities as well as choose to *believe* in your power to do it.

Next, as we express our faith or *intention* to create change, we gain control over our problem. This is the power behind our efforts. The more confidence we have in our ability to make the necessary changes, the more effective we'll be. Any small effort will produce an effect, but clarity, confidence, and focused *intention* are so much more powerful. We hold the power with our *intention* and desire in order to shift nearly anything that plagues us.

So, *choose* to make a specific change, *believe* in your power to influence your life, and exert focused *intention* to create!

Let's put all this into action. Here are some simple instructions so you know what to expect.

First, choose a problem. You might work on one of these areas:

- A physical pain — headache, stomachache, muscle stiffness, etc.

- A limiting belief — this defines your identity ("I'm worthless," "I'm not loveable," "I am ugly," "I'm not successful")

- A negative thought — the mean voices in your head ("No one wants me around," "I'll never know my purpose," "I'll never be happy" — anything that's trying to squash your greatness)

- A negative emotion — anger, fear, anxiety, or whatever you are feeling that weighs you down or keeps you from moving forward

- A painful memory — usually an experience that was too much to handle in the moment, so you brushed it aside (Unfortunately, it doesn't leave; it just gets stored away somewhere inside you to cause problems later.)

Second, rate the intensity of this problem on a scale. Imagine a number from 1-10 that helps you give a numeric value to how bad you're feeling. You need to reference this initial intensity after using the technique so you can more easily notice how much it's shifted.

Finally, as you think about the problem, go through each of the words HEAL, ADDRESS/STRENGTHEN, REMOVE, RELEASE and RESTORE. Again, these words don't have power in and of themselves; they get their power from our desires and focused intentions.

After you say each word, take a deep breath. Breathing is an important step in the beginning. It will help you recognize the shift more clearly.

As you move through the technique, you may feel the intensity decrease quickly or just begin to shift. It might shift a little or a lot. The more energy and focus you can put toward each step, the more effective it will be and the faster you'll see results.

Let's do this together. Choose a physical challenge, a belief, a thought, an emotion, or the pain of a memory that you want to eliminate. Now, hold it in your mind.

What are you feeling? How would you rate this intensity on a scale of 1-10?

At this point I want you to say to yourself the word HEAL and take a deep breath.

- During this process, you are literally asking your body to shift into healing mode.
- You're holding the intention that anything in your body that needs to heal physically has the focus of your entire being.
- Feel the intensity begin to shift.

Now say the word ADDRESS or STRENGTHEN and breathe.

- You're asking for those things inside you that need to be stronger to wake up and help you resolve this issue.
- Feel your body getting stronger.

Next, say to yourself REMOVE and breathe.

- You're telling anything negative hanging around to leave.
- They are not welcome, and you're making them go.
- This negativity cannot stay inside of or around you if you tell it to leave.

Next, say RELEASE and take a nice deep breath.

- If you're thinking about heavy feelings, negative thoughts, or limiting beliefs, this is where you really get focused.
- Breathe the air all the way out.

Last, say the word RESTORE and take another deep breath.

- Imagine letting go of any programming that doesn't serve you.

- This one's like hitting the reset button for a fresh start.
- Feel the intensity going down — all the way down.

Sit quietly for a moment and take note of the experience. Recognize and record the changes. How intense is your problem? Has it calmed down? Has it seemed to move? For example, were you focusing on a stiff neck and now it's moved to an ache in your left shoulder? Or were you worried about making your house payment and now you're feeling like you're not good enough to give that presentation in a meeting tomorrow? It's important to recognize your progress and take notes, so you can record your *eureka* moment. Record the thoughts or feelings that came.

So, what do you do next? If the intensity dropped, great job. Repeat the technique until it's gone. If the problem seemed to move, that's good too. It actually resolved and your next problem is ready to go. Whatever it is, it's perfect. Trust that your journey is perfect. Your body will start letting you know what's ready to heal. Be ready for it.

CHAPTER 23

MAKING IT REAL

*"With everything that has happened to you,
you can either feel sorry for yourself or treat what
has happened as a gift. Everything is either an
opportunity to grow or an obstacle to keep you
from growing; you get to choose."*

~ *Wayne Dyer*

Let's review for a minute about how to make these tools work for you. What good is a technique that you can't replicate or really apply to your real life challenges? There are several obstacles that may block you from implementing these simple, powerful tools. Just remembering can be difficult. Something may whisper to you that it really can't work for you or that it can't be that easy or even that it's too hard to use in the moment when you're struggling with something. I understand. Adding in a new habit to a busy life can be tricky, but it is possible.

You may be missing activities that you once enjoyed. What if you could find your way back to them? If there's something you want badly enough, you'll find a way to remember. One of my students really likes cooking but with her several health concerns she couldn't stand for more than a couple minutes before the pain started creeping in. Her back and feet would scream at her so she would have to sit down. After learning these techniques, she was standing in the kitchen cooking something and started feeling the pain build up. She stopped for a minute, used the simple techniques, and the pain calmed down. She was able stand as long as she needed to finish cooking. This may not be profound, but for her it was almost miraculous.

Instead of thinking about all the ways that it can't or won't work, how about shifting any thinking of that sort to "How can I make this work for me?" Just that small shift can open up all kinds of mechanisms inside of you to help you figure out how to make it work. Remember, every thought you have carries a vibration with it that your body responds to. Do you want it resonating with a limiting belief that prevents you from taking advantage of this great technique? Change that pattern now if it's one you struggle with. Set yourself up for success.

Let's discuss how you can you remember to use HEAL, AD-DRESS/STRENGTHEN, REMOVE, RELEASE and RE-STORE in your life? What do you do to remind yourself of other things you need to do? A reminder on your phone? Post-it notes around the house? Accountability partners? You'll see that all of your efforts will be worthwhile and these words will be there when you need them.

There's also something to be said for simply setting the intention to let these tools help you in your life—just that basic step can help trigger the awareness when you need them. Asking yourself "How can it work?" is the first step. Choose to include it in your toolbox of self-care.

Negative thoughts are another obstacle to making real change in our lives. They can come from inherited or imprinted programming or even bad guys. Those thoughts could tell you that you can't really change or find relief. They could also say that these techniques are too simple; they can't possibly work. Start here if necessary. Use the techniques to eliminate everything that tries to stop you before you even start. I experienced several significant mental obstacles. A seemingly endless string of negative thoughts tried to prevent me from healing and dreaming. What I found is that working through the technique for every obstacle that surfaces works the best.

Not only can you use this technique in reaction to things that come up, but you can work proactively on problems before they are triggered. A helpful tip is to make an action list or a list of priorities that you want to work on. In a moment of struggle, it can be difficult to think clearly enough to say a word and breathe. As you work through your action lists, however, you do two things: first, you experience success during good times which helps you use these techniques with confidence when things get hard; and second, you diminish the reactivity within you so that when you do face a challenge you won't be immediately overcome. You will have a space where you can choose how you want to react. This is where you can calm yourself and heal what needs to be healed and react how you wish you would react.

Lets begin by making a list. What are the triggers in your life that send you for a loop? Just think about that person that stretches your patience or that situation that overwhelms you. Think about when someone cuts you off in traffic on your drive home from a stressful day at work. What about that new puppy that's tearing up your nice furniture? Then there's that old flame that hurt you twenty years ago and for some reason still stings when you remember him or her. You can feel a deep reaction, can't you? You can use the same method outlined above to rate the intensity of that feeling and then work it down. The more you use these techniques proactively, the more they will be in the forefront of your mind and have a chance of being recalled when you need them.

What are the options? If you're reading this book and you've hung on this long, you likely really need these tools. You've put this much effort into helping yourself out of your challenges, so don't stop now—put it all to work and watch in amazement.

Keep going. You've been given a beautiful gift that can help you resolve so many of your concerns. Commit to the implementation of this new path; you will be so glad that you did!

CHAPTER 24

KEEPING IT REAL

"We delight in the beauty of the butterfly,
but rarely admit the changes it has gone through
to achieve that beauty."

~ *Maya Angelou*

Even deeper than the negative thoughts that make it hard for us to change is the internal programming that creates them. This programming can either be inherited or imprinted and its sole purpose is to keep us safe. A friend of mine, Coach Sean Smith illustrates this concept in a great way. Imagine that you are in a secure compound, a "safe zone." Patrolling the walls are specialized "security guards" who are there for your protection. The only problem? Their definition of an actionable threat is not when something dangerous tries to get *in* but when you want to go *out* and try something new—when you start to grow.

You may have experienced these internal-programming "security guards" before, for example, when you started taking steps toward your dreams. Their only job is to keep us safe from pain, disappointment, fear, or something really crazy like personal growth and achieving goals. The moment we start trying to leave the safety zone, they do whatever it takes to pull us down and bring us back—for our own good, of course.

This self-preservation can take various shapes:

1. An illness or random pain showing up out of nowhere
2. Your family suddenly acting up or arguing
3. You lose your job
4. Plain old fear grips your life and tries to shut you down

A student of mine had an interesting experience once. She was feeling sick for a few days but was then beginning to feel better—all but her voice. When she called me, she still didn't have much of a voice. She was basically whispering when we got on the phone. She said she had worked on it for about 3 days but then she couldn't anymore. We realized that I actually needed to work on it for her. I had been teaching her as I was learning, but she didn't have the latest information that would enable her to identify her struggles and work through them herself. Once I identified it, I was able to share it with her and her voice immediately began to improve. We both worked on that marker for her for a few minutes and then we realized that her voice was coming back. It only took about 5 minutes and her voice completely returned. This one contributor to her voice weakness was directly related to her using her voice to speak up for what she believes in. She needed to become aware of this obstacle and the message behind it in order to finish healing and move on.

The self-preservation offered up can be anything that halts our progress or causes us anxiety about the new direction we're heading to improve our situation. My advice is to recognize it when it comes, learn the lessons, and as necessary, put on your fighting boots—they can be the red high-heeled type like a friend of mine envisions or maybe steel-toed combat boots—whatever your style is.

So what does it look like to win this battle? Recognize that you are not your issue. Sometimes we take on our challenge as if it is our new identity. Don't get sucked in to believing that *you* are the illness, stress, failure, or fear. It is just a lesson that is showing up to test how committed you are to this new path.

You have new tools to be able to respond to anything that comes up. It doesn't matter whether it is lower back pain, frustration with a co-worker, fear of getting in front of people, or the haunting of a traumatic memory that ails you. These simple, powerful tools can get you through it all. Be patient and persistent and you will see beautiful results.

Be ready to use your new tools at a moment's notice. Use these techniques as soon as you see the slightest sign of an issue. Don't wait until you're fuming at your family for yet another disagreement; keep your head cool and calm so that you can think clearly and logically to resolve things that come up before they get to that point. If you know that you're going to *that* restaurant with your friends tonight, work on your digestive system to get it ready to respond to your challenging meal. If you can see far enough ahead or know that you have a trigger coming up, work on it before the problem arises.

Share this book with a friend so you can have a teammate who'll have your back and help you see through the darkness. It's great to have support when you make a significant shift in your life. Surely one of your family members or friends is ready to up-level like you're doing. Include them in your journey so that you can help each other through the challenges and succeed together. Whether you are looking to tackle a physical pain, lessen or eliminate sweet tooth cravings, going for a new level in your business, or just wanting to feel more peace in your life, connect with someone on a similar journey and support each other to move above the line and live great.

You're ready!

Chapter 25

Up-leveling

"There are only two ways to live your life.
One is as though nothing is a miracle.
The other is as though everything is a miracle."

~ Albert Einstein

Now that you have seen how to apply this work, let's up-level your healing ability. Once you are comfortable with using each of the words, it may start feeling a bit cumbersome. At this point you may wonder a thing or three like, "Do I need to go through each of the words each time I struggle with something?" Or "How do I know if I need HEAL, AD-DRESS/STRENGTHEN, REMOVE, RELEASE or RE-STORE?" Or "Can I mess something up?"

First of all, don't worry. You can't mess anything up here. You can't hurt yourself with these techniques. Your body knows how it needs to heal; you simply provide the direction for the energy to get it done. Sometimes as you resolve one problem, another will show up that's been waiting in the wings or that was quiet enough that you didn't notice it. That's perfect. You didn't do anything wrong; on the contrary, you're making progress and can move on to the next issue.

Second, you don't have to go through all the words individu-ally forever. Once you understand each word, you can actually combine them to use all at once. You can shorten this technique to the acronym "HARRR." It will work as long as the meaning is not lost. In this way, you don't have to worry about using the right word for any given issue because you're using all of them at once and affecting all five angles at the same time. In this way, it speeds up your efforts so that you can resolve problems faster; however, it's still your choice. You can keep using the individual words if you prefer.

Now that you have a new shortcut, let's go through the technique again.

First, choose a challenge that you want to eliminate.

- Do you have any of that headache or frustration left from before?
- How about any thoughts like, "I can't do this" or "This will work on everyone but me" or "My problem is too much to resolve like this."
- Are you still struggling with anxiety about your future, regret about the past, or fear to step into your greatness?
- Let's get rid of those, shall we?

Next, rate the new problem—or new intensity of the earlier problem. What is the intensity on a scale of 1-10?

Now, take your problem and its rating and apply your new shortcut to the technique. Take a deep breath and jump in.

Say to yourself the word HARRR and take a deep breath.

- You've up-leveled your efforts.
- Feel the intensity shifting

Say HARRR again and breathe.

- Stay focused on what you are trying to shift.

- The more senses you involve, the more effective you'll be. Think about it, feel it, visualize it, maybe hear it as well if it helps you to focus.

One more time, say HARRR and breathe.

- Use your inner strength to invite healing from every angle.
- You have the power to help your body heal—believe it!
- Notice the intensity going down the scale—all the way down

Wonderful! Think about your problem—how is it now? How far has the intensity come down? Did you notice it dropping faster than the first time? Is it completely gone?

Fantastic. Just like the last time, repeat this technique as many times as you'd like. Commit to yourself to work through your challenges and get them down to manageable levels or even eliminated. You can do this. It's effective for any issue, at anytime, anywhere you are—take control of your life with this simple yet powerful tool.

When doing this work, here are some key points to remember:

1. When an issue is healed, it's gone.
2. If it seems to come back, it's likely one of two things: another layer of the same issue manifesting itself or an entirely different problem taking advantage of a weak spot.
3. Some problems take more time than others. Be patient and consistent, as the apparent delay in healing could be part of your perfect journey too.
4. Be patient with yourself as you increase your skill with healing. One of my students found it very difficult to sit for more than a couple of minutes to focus on healing something. After sticking with it for a while, he not

only resolved many issues, but he has also built up his endurance for working on himself and his family. He can now sit for 30-40 minutes to focus his healing efforts. This is not always necessary, but when it is, powerful healing occurs.

CHAPTER 26

VIBRATIONAL GOAL SETTING

*"No problem can be solved from the same
level of consciousness that created it."*

~ Albert Einstein

Now that you have new techniques to use to respond to health and life challenges, let's move you from survival mode below the line to creation mode *above the line*. Put your new skills to work for you to help you achieve you goals. The same obstacles that cause you pain, frustration, or feelings of worthlessness are the same obstacles that can prevent you from accomplishing your dreams. It is greatly a matter of vibration. The five words HEAL, ADDRESS/STRENGTHEN, REMOVE, RELEASE and RESTORE all raise your vibration.

In order to resolve challenges, we must raise our vibration to the level at which its solutions reside. What this tells us is that the solutions to our problems lie within our reach as we clear the obstacles to living healthy physical, vibrational, energetic, and social lives. In addition to working on the regular obstacles and removing them so we can effectively move toward our goals, we must be sure to raise our vibrations as well.

Here's an example. When we moved into our home, the wheel on the back corner of the bottom rack of the dishwasher was missing, making it difficult to roll in and out. I struggled each time I used it but didn't think there was anything I could do to fix it. Maybe once or twice I had a very brief thought that maybe it would help to move a less important wheel to that crucial back position. For some reason, I quickly dismissed the thought each time. Perhaps it wasn't ever strong enough to capture my attention and really consider the option. Or maybe I wasn't ready for a proactive solution. Either way, I simply moved on, frustrated at the difficulty.

One day, I had the thought again but this time I stopped what I was doing and genuinely considered a possible solution. I decided it was worth a try, so I removed a wheel near the front of the rack and moved it to the vacant back position. I pushed the rack back into the machine and it easily rolled in. I was shocked—and a little irritated at myself for not taking the time to do that earlier.

Months of frustration and the whole solution only took about a minute and a half. The whole scene got me wondering: How did that happen? Why now? Why was I willing to at least try a possible solution at this moment in time but I wasn't before? I sat and thought about that for a few minutes and decided it was a matter of vibration. I realized that it was my thoughts, beliefs, and emotions that determined my willingness to attend to the problem. Vibrations. The solution was always there; I just didn't recognize it fully. I realized that thanks to months and months of working on myself, I had reached a higher overall vibration, making me feel capable of dismissing the false/limiting belief that I couldn't fix it and thereby simply respond to the answer that came. The higher vibration facilitated the solution to the problem.

This simple story is not unique. Every day we face challenges and pursue goals, some of which we see solutions to and some we do not. The difference in our vision is our vibration. What I mean by this is that the reason you clearly see a solution is because your vibration has changed. You moved up the vibrational scale and now resonate with the solution you were seeking. You couldn't see it before but now you can. It may have even been there all along like in my dishwasher solution, but you didn't recognize it until now.

The big question then is how to replicate my dishwasher success with other challenges or goals? The answer: identify your goals and challenges and work toward being in a place to receive the answers. Work on yourself daily to keep raising your vibration so that you will eventually meet the resolutions and achieve your goals.

This work empowers us to heal the unseen factors that hold us back from living a *life above the line*—a life that resides and thrives in creation mode. As we apply these principles to our goals, challenges, dreams, fears, difficulties, and aspirations, we literally change who we are which increases our capacity to realize our amazing potential and causes the elements around us to reorganize for our good.

Set goals. Raise your vibration. Achieve your goals. Repeat.

CHAPTER 27

THE LIFE YOU'RE
MEANT TO LIVE

*"At the center of your being you have the answer; you
know who you are and you know what you want."*

~ *Lao Tzu*

I'm so excited for you. The next chapter in your life is just
beginning. This will be a chapter of growth, insights, empower-
ment, healing, and achievement. As you enter this new chapter,
you'll be faced with opportunities to overcome many of the obstacles that have held you back and kept you below the line. You
are preparing to move your *life above the line* and live in creation
mode. Take a deep breath.

These techniques have helped me see my own worth, my
gifts, and the ways that I am meant to serve the world. They've
cleared away the darkness that prevented me from seeing the *real*
me—the one that has great value to share. It was quite a journey
to begin seeing the good easily—it was pretty buried. I think it's
this way for many of us, if not all of us. At the end of the book,
you will find three worksheets designed to help you identify your
challenges, gifts, and goals. This process of discovery will help
you in your quest to live your *life above the line* and become who
you are meant to become.

Life can condition us to see our weaknesses more easily than we see our possibilities. We're more inclined to declare our weaknesses for everyone to know than to share with someone our strengths, gifts, or abilities. We're often worried about making someone else feel badly if we've done well at something. Lately, society seems to be praising the mediocre and bashing the exceptional.

I love that oft-shared quote by Marianne Williamson from her book Return to Love:

> *Our deepest fear is not that we are inadequate. Our deepest fear is that we are powerful beyond measure. It is our light, not our darkness that most frightens us. We ask ourselves, 'Who am I to be brilliant, gorgeous, talented, fabulous?' Actually, who are you not to be? You are a child of God. Your playing small does not serve the world. There is nothing enlightened about shrinking so that other people won't feel insecure around you. We are all meant to shine, as children do. We were born to make manifest the glory of God that is within us. It's not just in some of us; it's in everyone. And as we let our own light shine, we unconsciously give other people permission to do the same. As we are liberated from our own fear, our presence automatically liberates others.*

This is what we should be celebrating in society, in our homes, and with each other. If we looked at ourselves the way a loving parent or teacher would look at us, our ability to handle challenges in life would increase and our worth would be clear and powerful just because we were born, and we would seek to expand our gifts so that we could serve the world and bless those around us.

You're worth every good thing that can come to you. Take that leap and go for your dreams. Everything that needs to heal inside of you in order to achieve those dreams will present itself. As this happens, recognize that message as an indicator that it is ready to be resolved. You will be able to heal and overcome every obstacle that surfaces in this manner. This journey of growth is exactly what you need right now. I honor you for hearing and accepting the call. It's your time to live the life you're meant to live—to live your *life above the line.*

"The things you are passionate about are not random, they are your calling."

~Fabienne Fredrickson

APPENDIX

Life Above The Line Worksheet

In *life above the line*, the Line represents the threshold between surviving and thriving, or between survival mode and creation mode. Let's do a little inventory together. The purpose here is to give you a tool to help you consider what may be keeping you in survival mode and then to explore what your life might look like in creation mode—living your *life above the line*. Here are a few questions—and prompts—to help facilitate some self-discovery. Open up here, get real, and get something to write on. No one's watching.

Under the Line, we experience struggle.

1. What is frustrating you the most in your life right now—physically, mentally, or emotionally?

- Do you struggle with back pain or headaches?
- What about focus or stress issues?
- Are you burdened by anxiety or sadness?

2. What would you love to see happen?

- Would you like a bit more energy?
- Do you want to feel more peace in your life?
- Would you like to accomplish a goal you've been working toward for too long?

3. What would be different in your life if you made that happen?

- Would you feel happier or more content with your life?
- Could you take time for your own needs without feeling guilty?
- Would you feel more capable of finishing necessary tasks each day?

4. What are you willing to do to have a new reality?
- Are you willing to change?
- Can you look honestly at the things that are holding you back?
- Can you commit to using a simple technique to steadily eliminate them?

5. Do you believe it's possible?
- Why or why not?
- If not, do you think it's a limitation inside of you or do you see external obstacles?
- If you see the obstacles as external, are you willing to work on what's inside of you anyway?
- Are you willing to see the possibility of a new reality?

Above the Line, we experience joy.

1. What do you want to accomplish in your life?
- Do you want more education? Maybe finish a degree?
- Do you want to change careers to one that you love?
- Do you want to run a marathon?

2. Do you believe you have a special purpose to fulfill?
- Did you know that you have gifts and talents that you are given in order to bless the world?
- Do you know what they are?

- How are you meant to serve the world?

3. How close are you to reaching your goals?

- What do you need in order to make them happen?
- Is something holding you back?
- What will your life be like when you're on that path to accomplishing them?

4. What will your life be like when you achieve your goal or are living your purpose?

- Have you allowed yourself to consider it?
- What would it feel like?
- What will you be like?
- What will you do next?

Work through these questions to discover and heal all of the *under the line* challenges and facilitate all of the *above the line* pursuits. As we change within, our world will change without. Amazing!

DISCOVERING GIFTS AND PURPOSE WORKSHEET

Now let's explore your gifts, focusing even more on your *life above the line*. Below are a few questions and prompts to get you going. Take time to really consider them and honestly respond.

Too often we dismiss the importance of what we are good at; what we have a knack for. We get tricked into believing that life must always be practical. We need to plan practically, we need to think practically, and we need to get a practical job. While that's great and all, I think the state of the people in our world has proven that practicality only goes so far. There needs to be a balance in the force.

We need people to discover and unleash their creativity, to think outside of the box more often, to explore solutions to our world's problems that don't make sense at first glance. That's when amazing things happen. Light bulbs are created, people fly to the moon, we can communicate with people on the other side of the world, and we can access incredible amounts of information at our fingertips.

What are your gifts?

1. What gifts, talents and abilities do you know you have?

- What are you good at?
- What you enjoy doing?
- You can spend hours on something and it feels like you barely got started. What is that thing?

- Give yourself credit for a minute. Be honest. This is your opportunity to open that door and take a good long look inside. You are amazing. What does your amazing look like?

2. What have people told you that you are good at?

- Remember some of those compliments. What were they?
- How did you respond? What did you think about them?
- Did you dismiss the compliments? Or did you recognize the truth?
- Take a look at yourself through your biggest fan's eyes. What are they seeing that you need to realize?

3. When you were a kid, what did you want to be when you grew up?

- Why? What was it about those professions or roles that drew you to them?
- How did they make you feel?
- What could you do to recreate that feeling?

4. What do you wish you were good at?

- Have you ever noticed someone doing something well and felt drawn to it?
- What have you tried and struggled at?
- If your fairy godmother could wave a magic wand and make you amazing at something, what would it be?

I've discovered that some of my greatest gifts were hidden behind my greatest weaknesses. So, let me ask you a question.

What weakness do you have?

- I know that may not sound helpful in this conversation, but just go with it. What things do you recognize that you struggle with?
- What big challenges have you had in your life? What challenges seem to repeat themselves?
- Considering these weaknesses, which ones are you currently working to overcome?

I hope that this has stirred your thinking. Let these questions simmer in you. Let their answers come. You'll learn things about yourself that you may never have considered.

So what is standing in your way? What obstacles are preventing you from unleashing your greatness? Just in case you're thinking, "Well, that's nice, but I don't know how to use my gifts even if I can see them." May I suggest that you shift that mindset? Instead, ask *how* you can use your gifts. Leave the door open for insights to come when they're ready. You may not know how to implement all of the beautiful things inside of you, but somewhere, at some point, the answers will come. Be ready.

You also have some new techniques that are at your disposal. They may appear deceptively simple, but don't discount their potential effect in your life. When questions, doubts, or obstacles get in your way, put the words and techniques that you learned here to work for you. Give them a real chance to improve your life, especially as you create a new powerful reality for yourself. You will be amazed.

You^X Exponential Worksheet

The purpose of this worksheet is to help you become who you are meant to become so that you can do what you're meant to do. Let's take a closer look at what you're made of. You have a treasure trove of gifts, talents, and abilities inside of you. Some are hidden and others you already love. They are all clues to help you to be happy, find success, and love your life. Follow the instructions below to begin uncovering your inner power.

For each of the following questions, write down as many things as you can think of. The more you record, the more complete your internal review will be.

YOU^X Exponential—becoming your exponential self

1. List your interests.

- What books are on your shelves?
- When you have free time, what do you go to first?
- What do you research online or read about in magazines?

Now prioritize your answers from what you enjoy to what you really love.

2. List your challenges.

- What are your biggest worries right now?
- What do you dread when you wake up in the morning?
- What nags at you throughout the day?

Now prioritize your answers from what you tolerate to what you really struggle with.

3. List your dreams.

- If time, money, and responsibilities were all taken care of, what would you do?
- If a genie gave you 3 wishes, what would they be? (the same freedoms as above)
- If you owned the perfect business right now, what would it be? What would it provide?

Now prioritize your answers from what you would like to do to what you would wake up for at 4am to get to do.

4. What is currently active in your life today?

- What do you see as your abilities?
- What are your talents?
- What gifts do you have that you'd love to serve the world with?

Now prioritize your answers from what activity you are tolerating to what you are so glad you are doing.

The lists that you have created from this questionnaire are your new starting point for living *life above the line*. As you look at your interests, remember that you can use these techniques to heal anything that holds you back from pursuing them. Likewise, with your challenges, you can heal all that prevents you from overcoming them. And with your goals, you can heal everything that keeps you from achieving them.

The lists can also work together. For example, with a specific interest, talent, or goal in mind, you can look at the list of challenges and ask which one is causing the most resistance and then work to heal it.

The applications to this work are limitless. When you work through the questions in these worksheets, imagine the increased power of your efforts to improve your life by applying the *Perfect*

Healing© mindset and skillset to heal all of the obstacles. You truly can achieve anything that you believe in your heart, so use what you know to heal—to improve what you truly believe. Then you can become who you're meant to become and do what you're meant to do.

This is the path to living a *life above the line*. Step by step, challenge after challenge, goal after goal, we seek to improve ourselves from within by working to heal all that stands in the way. The *Perfect Healing©* system is not a bull-in-a-china-shop mentality but rather that of a peaceful warrior who humbly and gratefully submits to the process. As we do so, untold abundance awaits.

"Becoming integrated and whole is the spiritual path. The body is your vehicle. Your job is to learn about yourself from your experiences and change yourself. This is spiritual growth."

~Gary Zukav

About the Author

Tiffany Garvin is an innovator in the field of self-healing and the human potential movement. She survived and thrived in an eighteen-year journey with chronic illnesses, the catalyst for her life's work. Her *Perfect Healing©* Master Course empowers people to heal their lives at every level so that they can be who they're meant to be and do what they're meant to do. Tiffany holds a Bachelor of Arts degree in Asian Studies/Chinese from Brigham Young University and is a first degree black belt in Kenpo Ju-jitsu. She is happily married, the mother of three children, and loves her life of writing, speaking, and healing.

For more information about the *Perfect Healing©* System, visit www.TiffanyGarvin.co.